Objects in Action

Commercial Applications of Object-Oriented Technologies

Paul Harmon and
David A. Taylor

with the assistance of
William Morrissey

ADDISON-WESLEY PUBLISHING COMPANY, INC.

Reading, Massachusetts • Menlo Park, California, • New York • Don Mills, Ontario
Wokingham, England • Amsterdam • Bonn • Paris • Milan • Madrid • Sydney
Singapore • Tokyo • Seoul • Taipei • Mexico City

Several of the figures that appear in Chapter 2 originally appeared in the *Object-Oriented Strategies* newsletter and are reproduced with the permission of Harmon Associates and Cutter Information.

The publisher offers discounts on this book when ordered in quantity for special sales. For more information please contact:

Corporate & Professional Publishing Group
Addison-Wesley Publishing Company
One Jacob Way
Reading, Massachusetts 01867

Library of Congress Cataloging-in-Publication Data

Harmon, Paul.
    Objects in action : commercial applications of object-oriented technologies / by Paul Harmon and David A. Taylor, with the assistance of William Morrissey.
       p.   cm.
    Includes index.
    ISBN 0-201-63336-1
    1. Object-oriented programming (Computer science). I. Taylor, David A., 1943– .
II. Morrissey, William. III. Title.
QA76.64.H365   1993
005.3—dc20
                                           93-4309
                                           CIP

Cover design by Simone R. Payment
Text design by Wilson Graphics & Design (Kenneth J. Wilson)
Set in 10 point Palatino by Impressions, a division of Edwards Brothers, Inc.

ISBN 0-201-63336-1

Text printed on recycled paper.
1 2 3 4 5 6 7 8 9 10-MU-96959493
First Printing, June 1993

TABLE OF CONTENTS

FOREWORD

The Object Management Group (OMG) was founded in 1989. The group is composed of an international assortment of hardware and software companies interested in promoting object-oriented technologies. The membership in OMG has grown steadily since its founding and is now approaching 300 members.

In keeping with its educational goals, in 1991 the OMG established Object World Inc. to arrange for educational briefings and to sponsor a commercial trade show on object technology. The first show, the Object World conference, was held in San Francisco in June of 1991. The second show was held in San Francisco in July of 1992.

In 1992, *Computerworld*, the weekly newspaper of information systems professionals, came to the OMG and suggested that it would be willing to sponsor a contest that would recognize outstanding applications that utilized object technology in conjunction with the 1992 Object World show. Applications were solicited during the Spring of 1992, judged in June, and awards were presented in July of 1992. The contest produced a surprising variety of applicants. The best applications illustrated that object technology is indeed being used by corporations and producing impressive results.

The winners in the five contest categories in 1992 were:

Category 1: Best Implementation of a Distributed Application Using OO Tools

Winner   Returns Processing Center Damaged Processing System, Kash n' Karry, Inc.

Runners-Up Custom Application Suite; Alain Pinel Realtors, Inc.; Total Benefit Administration; Hewitt Associates

Category 2: Best Implementation of a Reusable Development Environment for Company Deployment

Winner   LYMB, General Electric

Runners-Up Helios, Broussais University Hospital OOA Analyst, Boeing Defense and Space Group

Category 3: Best Object-Based Application Developed Using non-OO Tools

Winner   Software Configuration Management System, Landschaftsverband, Rheinland

Runners-Up	Linkup, Westinghouse Savannah River Company, Smelter Information System, Alumax Primary Division
Category 4:	Best Cost-Saving Implementation Using an Object Approach
Winner	CZ Protocol Print, Wacker Siltronic Corp.
Runners-Up	Gas Purchase Accounting and Administration, Southern California Gas Company; "Just the Facts," San Jose Police Department
Category 5:	Best Use of Object Technology within an Enterprise or Large Systems Environment
Winner	Concession Management, United Artists Theatre Circuit, Inc.
Runners-Up	Business and Management Support System, Civil Aviation Authority (UK), Order Management Network Integration System, Siemans Energy and Automation

What impressed everyone was that a review of all of the applications submitted revealed the rapidly growing and increasingly effective use of object technology. Several judges suggested that OMG ought to sponsor a book that would document the variety and quality of many of the contest applications.

To assure a wider audience for these early examples of the use of object technology, we asked Paul Harmon and David Taylor, two authors who have demonstrated skill in writing about object technology, to work with the developers of many of the applications submitted for the first *Computerworld*/Object World contest to document a number of the applications submitted in 1992. This book is the result of that effort.

We hope this book will provide corporate developers with some inspiration and with practical information about what is involved in developing applications that employ object technology.

Computerworld and Object World plan to sponsor another contest in 1993 to recognize new object-based applications that have been developed in the interval. We hope that a second edition of this book or a subsequent book will be prepared in due course so that corporate developers will be able to follow the rapid and impressive development of this major new development in the software industry.

Bill Hoffman, President
Object World Corporation,
Object Management Group

Gary J. Beach, Publisher
Computerworld

CHAPTER 1

BUILDING SOFTWARE OUT OF OBJECTS

INTRODUCTION

It is exciting to witness the advent of a new software technology that actually delivers on its promises. Unlike so many of the "silver bullets" of years past, object technology is proving itself in the field with reassuring regularity. In company after company, developers are finding that objects allow them to create new applications with surprising speed and ease. More importantly, these applications often contain functionality that would not have been feasible with conventional technologies. And the resulting applications are proving to be very flexible and extensible, reducing maintenance costs and helping companies keep pace with changing business requirements.

Those of us who have worked as consultants and analysts in this field have had the pleasure of seeing such results in many different companies. Unfortunately, much of what we see is confidential or unavailable to the public for other reasons, so not everyone gets to see the spectrum of successes that we do. It was to make these successes more visible that *Computerworld* and Object World sponsored the first annual Object Applications contest.

The response to this contest was quite gratifying. Companies from all over the world submitted their applications of object technology to a panel of judges with expertise in the field, a panel on which both authors were privileged to sit. As described in the Foreword, there were three finalists in each of five categories, with one winner named in each. Although this book is organized by different categories from those of the contest, we have included all five winners in the book together with eight of the other ten finalists. We have also included six additional entries that we regarded as particularly informative case studies.

To make it more convenient for readers to find applications of particular interest, we have structured the book in terms of five different application areas: manufacturing, software development, sales and service, government and utilities, administration, and medicine. We have provided brief introductions to each section to help set a context for understanding the problems that were tackled and the benefits that were achieved.

1

We have also included two introductory chapters to provide some generic background for reading about these applications. This first chapter summarizes the basic principles of object technology in a way that should be accessible to managers and developers alike. The second chapter analyzes how object technology is currently being applied in commercial environments. Either chapter may be read, skimmed, or skipped, depending on the reader's background and interests.

INTRODUCING OBJECTS

Object-oriented (OO) technology is based on a few simple concepts that, when combined, produce significant improvements in software construction. Unfortunately, the basic concepts of the technology often get lost in the excitement over advanced features or advantageous characteristics. It is for this reason that we have chosen to restate the basic ideas behind object technology here. Having done that, we explore some of the advanced features and then summarize the benefits of the technology.

The central concept behind object technology is, of course, that of the object. Briefly put, an object is a software package that contains related data and procedures. Although objects can be used for any purpose, they are most frequently used to represent real-world objects such as products, customers, and sales orders. The basic idea is to define software objects that can interact with each other just as their real-world counterparts do, modeling the way a business works and providing a natural foundation for building systems to manage that business. Exhibit 1.1 shows several objects interacting with each other to reflect the sale of a product.

The tight coupling of process and data in object technology is a unique quality. Throughout the history of software, we have made a sharp distinction between data and procedures. The two were developed according to two different principles, they were stored in different places, and they were usually maintained in different ways during and after the execution of a program.

This classic division made sense for the first generation of computers, in which procedures were implemented by wires in a plug board and data were maintained on punched tape or revolving magnetic drums. But over the years procedures and data have been getting closer to each other. Most modern languages form a tight bond between a specific set of data and the procedures that operate on those data, using "scoping rules" to make the data invisible to other procedures. Similarly, the current generation of database management systems (DBMSs) allows procedures to be stored directly in the database along with the data they manage. In each case, the primary organization of the software mimics the way the business is structured. The division between data and procedures is made only secondarily, after the primary units have been defined.

In a sense, then, object technology represents the culmination of a decades-long trend to bring related data and procedures together. In object technology,

Exhibit 1.1

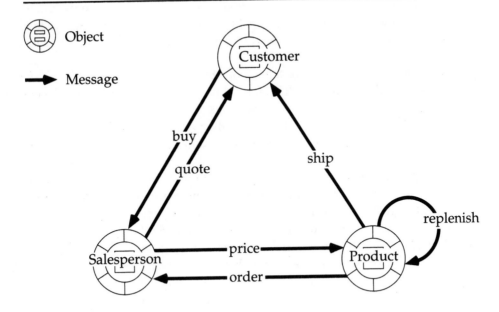

Object

Message

the packaging of related data and procedures into objects is called *encapsulation.* Encapsulation is a powerful technique for building better software because it provides neat, manageable units that can be developed, tested, and maintained independently of one another. In fact, in a fully object-oriented design, it is not possible to define procedures that are not bound to an object. For this reason, procedures are often called *methods* in object technology. This use of a new term emphasizes the fact that object-oriented procedures are different from conventional, free-standing functions.

Object technology takes the growing trend toward encapsulating data and procedures a step further—it strives to erase the distinction between the two altogether beyond the barriers of the object. With objects, we focus on how an object plays out its role in a larger context, leaving the distinction between process and data as an implementation detail. This technique is called *information hiding.* This is an unfortunate choice of terms because it conjures up images of bureaucratic secrecy and presidential cover-ups. But the idea here is not to hide valuable information from concerned outsiders, but to protect those who don't need to know from the burden of dealing with irrelevant details.

For example, suppose a product object is required to report its current retail price whenever it is asked for it. In conventional programming, the first thing we would do is decide whether the price was sufficiently stable to store it in a variable or so labile that we would have to calculate it on the fly whenever we needed it.

Then we would communicate our decisions to all the other procedures that might need to request the price. In effect, we would say, "If you need to know the price, check the value of the following variable, which is formatted in the following way," or, "If you need to know the price, call this function and it will calculate it for you."

With objects, we would not tell anyone else about how the value was determined. We would simply say, "If you need the current price, ask me." We would not bother them about whether it was in a variable and how it was formatted. This simplifies the job of other objects—all they have to know is how to ask—and it makes our software easier to change. For example, we could change the price from a variable to a calculation in response to changing business requirements. In a conventional system, such a change would immediately break all the communications concerning price. In an object system, everything would continue to work just as it did before because the information about whether a value was stored or calculated was hidden from everyone outside the product object.

Exhibit 1.2 shows the internal organization of an individual object. As the illustration suggests, all access to the object's variables is through its methods, ensuring that no other objects are even aware of this object's internal structure. By the way, some languages allow a developer to bypass this mechanism and declare variables as public entities. However, doing so throws away some of the valuable benefits of information hiding because making this information public causes other objects to depend on it.

Exhibit 1.2

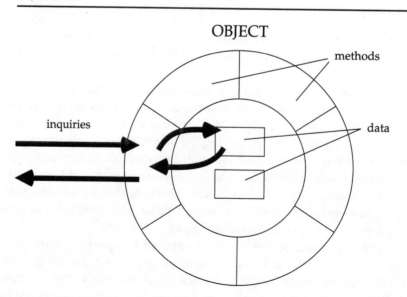

CLASSES AS TEMPLATES FOR OBJECTS

In principle, packaging data and procedures together makes perfect sense. In practice, it raises an awkward problem. Suppose we have many objects of the same general type—for example, a thousand product objects, each of which could report its current price. Any data these objects contained could easily be unique for each object. Stock number, price, storage dimensions, stock on hand, reorder quantity, and other values would differ from one product to the next. But the methods for dealing with these data might well be the same. Do we have to copy these methods and duplicate them in every object?

No. This would be ridiculously inefficient, and all object-oriented languages provide a simple way of capturing these commonalities in a single place. That place is called a *class,* and it acts as a kind of template for objects of a similar nature. For example, we could define a class called product that would define all the generic characteristics of the various products a company needed to deal with, now or in the future. These characteristics would include two kinds of things: method definitions and variable definitions. All that is required of the actual objects—which are called *instances* of the class—is to store the actual values of the variables. Exhibit 1.3 shows the relationship between the class and its instances.

Exhibit 1.3

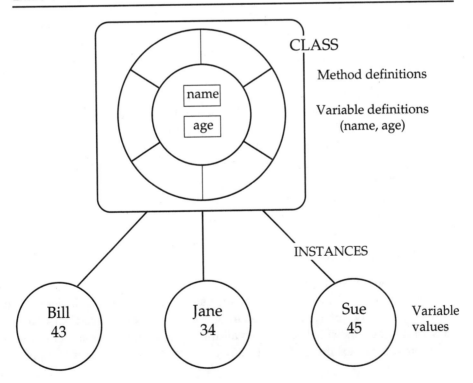

In short, a class is a template for objects. Once you define the template, you can stamp out as many objects (instances of the class) as you like. Each can take on different values, but all use the same variables and work with the same methods. This is how you can have a thousand different product objects but only define the method for computing the price in one place.

RELATIONSHIPS AMONG CLASSES

Objects, as defined by their classes, are the fundamental building blocks for all object-oriented software. The next step in understanding object technology is to explore how objects are connected together to form working systems. This is an easy task because there are only three ways that objects can be connected together:

1. Specialization, in which one object is a special case of another object.
2. Composition, in which one object contains another object.
3. Collaboration, in which one object requests a service from another object.

Actually, all three relationships are defined in terms of classes, not objects. Remember, classes provide the generic definitions for different kinds of objects, which are created at runtime actually to carry out the work of a system. Because specialization, composition, and collaboration apply to all the objects belonging to a given class, they are defined in the class rather than being repeated within every object.

In the following sections we describe each of the three relationships in turn. As we do, bear in mind that we are talking about the structure of all software, including programs and databases. This is part of the breakthrough aspect of object technology. Because the basic distinction between data and procedures is hidden as much as possible, a single set of design principles can be applied to both programs and databases. No longer do you design the two separately, then figure out how to get them together and keep them in harmony. Instead, you design a single object model that encompasses both data and procedures. Then, almost as an afterthought, you decide which data need to be maintained over time and add methods to store these in a database.

1. Specialization

One of the unusual aspects of object technology is that units of software can be defined as special cases of each other, using the software equivalent of "it's just the same only different." By declaring one class to be a special case, or subclass, of another, the subclass inherits all the method and variable definitions of its superclass. For example, if we declare a printer to be a subclass of a product,

Exhibit 1.4

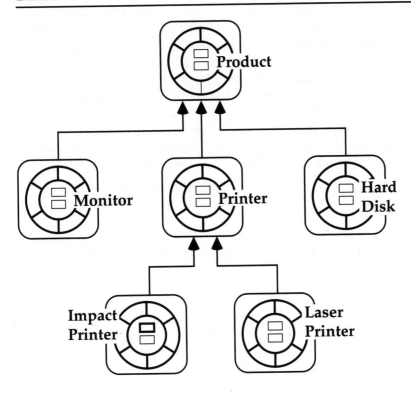

then printer objects automatically have methods and variables for dealing with generic things such as reporting their current price and reordering themselves. The printer class, in turn, could add methods and variables that were specific to printers such as knowing what replacement cartridges fit the machine and how many pages it could print per minute.

This specialization can be carried to any number of levels, defining what is termed a *class hierarchy*. Exhibit 1.4 shows a partial class hierarchy for computer peripherals. In this example, a laser printer would inherit all the method and variable definitions from product and from printer, adding its own definitions to capture the characteristics that are unique to laser printers.

2. Composition

Classes can also be defined as components of one another. For example, a laser printer might contain, among many other components, a print engine, a roller, a print cartridge, a paper tray, and perhaps one or more font cartridges.

Composition provides a convenient means of capturing the fact that these parts all go together, and it allows them to be treated as a single collective entity.

Composition is especially useful for defining high-level objects that can hide the details of their inner workings. As illustrated in Exhibit 1.5, a division might consist of a specified set of departments, several divisions could be combined into a business unit, and a company might include any number of business units. Being able to capture high-level concepts like these is very important in building business systems. For example, a company object could interact with all of its component business units without having to know anything about the internals of those business units. If it needed the current operating budget for a given business unit, it would simply request it. It would know nothing about how the business unit queried each of its divisions, which queried their departments in turn to roll up the total budget. This is another case of information hiding at work, simplifying an otherwise complex system.

It is important not to confuse specialization with composition: they have different properties and serve different functions. For example, the hierarchy defined

Exhibit 1.5

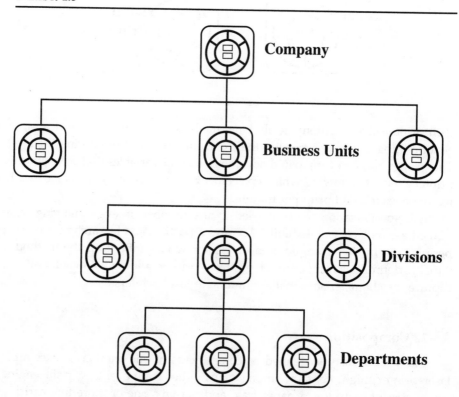

by an organization (Exhibit 1.5) is not an inheritance hierarchy. Departments do not inherit properties from divisions, and divisions do not inherit from business units. That is because they are components of one another, not special cases of each other.

3. Collaboration

The two relationships we have examined so far are static in nature. We could define a hundred classes, fit them into neat specialization and composition hierarchies, and throw them into a program and absolutely nothing would happen. We need one more kind of relationship, one that triggers objects into action. That is where collaboration comes in.

A *collaboration* between two objects is a request from one object to another to carry out one of its services. The request takes the form of a message from the first object, called the *sender*, to the second object, called the *receiver*. The message consists of the name of a method defined by the receiver together with any information, expressed as parameters or arguments, that the receiver needs to carry out that method. Exhibit 1.6 illustrates a sales order requesting the current price from a product, passing the quantity so that the product can calculate any volume discounts that might apply.

Collaborations provide the active element in object technology. The other two relationships, important as they are, are merely packaging rules that define how objects are composed. It is the passing of messages among objects during the execution of a program that actually makes the objects carry out their tasks.

Exhibit 1.6

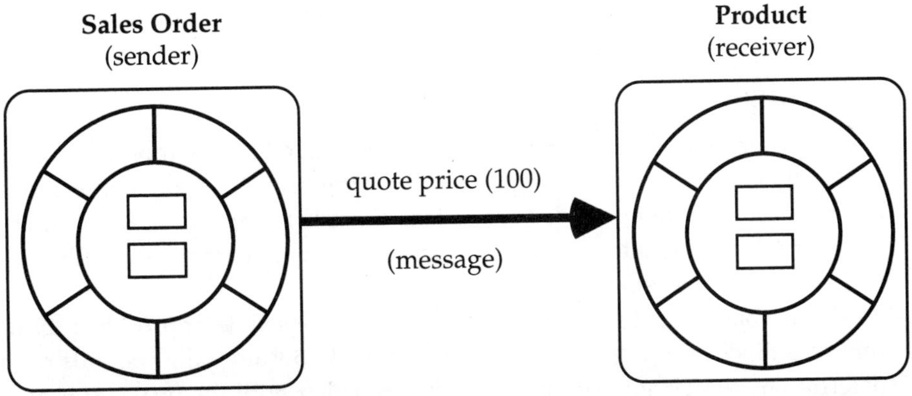

Sales Order
(sender)

Product
(receiver)

quote price (100)

(message)

ADVANCED FEATURES

These three relationships define all the ways that objects can be connected to form larger structures. As such, they tell you everything you need to know to understand how object-oriented software works. However, in clarifying the basic relationships we glossed over some subtler aspects of object technology that are important to understanding its benefits. One of the most important of these goes by the unwieldy name of polymorphism.

Polymorphism

Polymorphism is a Greek term meaning "many forms." It is used to express the fact that the same message can be sent to many different objects and interpreted in different ways by each object. For example, we could send the message "replenish yourself" to many different kinds of product objects. They would all respond to the same message, but they might do so in very different ways. For products that a company buys intact and redistributes, all that might be involved is selecting the vendor and generating a purchase order for the economic order quantity. For products that are manufactured on site, a much more complex chain of events might take place, including messages to the master production schedule to put more of the products into production. For still other products, orders might be placed with other factories to produce the required quantity.

The important point is that we can use generic method names and allow each object to interpret them differently, depending on the object's own unique needs. This greatly simplifies the structure of software. No longer do we have to include complex "switch" or "branch" statements in programs to figure out what function to call based on what kind of thing is being operated on. We simply send a standard message to whatever object we need a service from. We do not have to specify how that service is performed. Indeed, we do not even need to know what kind of object is receiving the message. All we care about is sending the right message; it's up to the receiver to interpret the request and do the correct thing.

Dynamic Binding

The concept of dynamic binding is closely related to polymorphism. In most conventional programming languages, all of the "calls" among subroutines are determined when the program is written. There is no provision for adding new kinds of subroutines later to meet new needs. This arrangement is usually referred to as *static* or *compile-time binding*.

Most object-oriented languages allow a more flexible approach to building software. Since the sender of a message does not know anything about its receiver, determining the identity of that receiver can be left until the program is actually running. This arrangement is known as *dynamic* or *runtime binding*. The advantage of dynamic binding is that it leaves all your options open until the moment the message is actually sent. In fact, you can make fundamental changes in the way a system works simply by adding new kinds of objects, without recompiling any programs or modifying existing classes.

For example, you could add a new product that had an entirely different approach to replenishing itself, such as a service product that knew how to assemble a fresh team of experts to provide the requested service. To add this new kind of product, all you would have to do is define it and drop it into your system. The fact that you never even conceived of selling services when you first built your system is irrelevant. Nothing in your system precluded selling services. All you have to do is add objects that know how to handle the special characteristics of services and you're in business.

BENEFITS OF OBJECT TECHNOLOGY

There is much more to object technology than this brief survey has conveyed, but it suffices to outline some of the benefits of the technology. These benefits come in two different flavors: benefits to the people who develop software, and benefits to the people who use it.

Benefits to Developers

The key benefits for developers are these:

- Faster development
- Increased quality
- Easier maintenance
- Enhanced modifiability

Many technologies have promised breakthroughs in the speed of software development. Few have delivered more than a 5 or 10% improvement. Object technology has now proven itself capable of delivering speed improvements ranging from a hundred to over a thousand percent. One of the authors of this book has reported 18 commercial case studies in which development time was cut by a factor of two to five, with one case returning a fourteen-to-one reduction (Taylor, *Object-Oriented Information Systems*). You will find further demonstrations of increased productivity in the present volume.

It is important to recognize where the added speed comes from. Programming with objects is not faster than other kinds of programming. The speed comes not from programming faster but from programming less. The critical factor is to build up an inventory of reusable class definitions such that new applications can be constructed largely by recombining existing classes. The more reuse you can achieve, the greater the benefit. For example, if 90% of a new application consists of existing classes, you can realize an order-of-magnitude reduction in development time.

Such reuse does not come free. It takes planning and investment. Faster development comes about not from adopting object technology, but from a systematic program of reuse. The technology is simply a vehicle for making this degree of reuse possible.

Increases in quality are largely a byproduct of this program of reuse. If 90% of a new application consists of proven, existing components, then only the remaining 10% of the code has to be tested from scratch. That observation implies (but does not guarantee) an order-of-magnitude reduction in defects. Further reductions can be achieved by using classes as the basis for extensive unit testing, thus ensuring the reliability of all components before they are combined into larger assemblies.

The increased ease of maintenance comes from several sources. First, if you only have 10% as many defects to begin with, you have a lot fewer bugs to chase down after the software is in the field. Second, the encapsulation and information hiding provided by objects serves to eliminate many kinds of defects and make others easier to find. For example, if there is a problem with the customer balance, you probably do not have to look any further than the methods and data of the customer class. Finally, any repairs you do make have less of a ripple effect because they are isolated by the affected objects. This means you no longer create ten new bugs for each one you eliminate.

Object-oriented software is easier to modify for the same reason. Because changes are neatly encapsulated, you can alter a system in rather fundamental ways without ever breaking it. Polymorphism and dynamic binding, described in the preceding section, are particularly valuable here. As the examples illustrated, it is actually possible to make old software handle requirements that did not even exist at the time the system was conceived simply by adding new kinds of objects.

This last benefit may well be the most important. The surest way to reduce the time and costs of software development is to eliminate it entirely. If we can build systems that are capable of evolving over time, then we can finally break the accelerating spiral in which software is constantly rebuilt from scratch to meet ever-changing needs.

Benefits to Consumers

To date, most claims for benefits of object technology have focused on the developers of the software, not the consumers of that software. For software development companies, the development benefits described above are sufficient motivation to adopt object technology. Similarly, non-software companies that construct their own information systems realize the same benefits because they are functioning as internal software developers.

But there is an additional set of benefits that can accrue to the end users of software that is quite different from the benefits realized by developers. Many software development companies have tried to suggest that object-oriented programs are inherently superior, but this is not necessarily the case. It is possible to build a wonderfully elegant system faster and better than ever before with objects and still deliver lousy software to end users. What matters to consumers is not how a program is structured, how long it took to create, or how hard it was to get the bugs out of it. What matters is what the program does and whether it helps users do their jobs faster, easier, and with higher quality.

Curiously, the issue of end-user benefits is largely ignored in most discussions of object technology. But there is a growing awareness that object technology can allow companies to build systems that actually improve the way they do business. Machine objects can be responsible for their own care and maintenance, ensuring that the real machines they represent never go without essential services. Similarly, order objects can take themselves through all the necessary steps to ensure that products are acquired and delivered on time, eliminating human labor that costs money, consumes time, and invites errors. And budget objects can roll themselves up from their components, whatever those may be, without human intervention. Just as important, they can break themselves back down into those same components on demand, providing automatic drill-down from any level at any time.

We like to think of these business benefits as the "second wave" of object technology. Important as the development benefits are, it is the business benefits that will ultimately produce the largest return on investment. Fortunately, the second wave is building rapidly, as the case studies in this book reveal. Although productivity benefits were often foremost in the minds of the developers who created these systems, a consistent subtheme running through this volume is that adopting object technology led to new insights into the business process and yielded daily operating benefits that might never have been realized with conventional technologies.

CHAPTER 2

THE USES OF OBJECT-ORIENTED PRODUCTS

Corporations and their information systems groups are faced with a rapidly changing business environment and are under pressure to solve a number of computer system problems: to reduce their costs, to use their computing resources more effectively and efficiently, to reduce the backlog of applications waiting to be developed, to reduce the time and resources required to maintain existing applications, to create new strategic applications as rapidly as they are needed, and to make the data within their systems available to managers and other end users whenever they need it. Put in the terms of the popular jargon, the major IS themes of the early 1990s are Re-engineering, Downsizing, Open Systems, Client-Server Systems, and the Strategic Use of Information Systems. The technology that most companies now hope to use to accomplish these goals is object-oriented technology.

There have, of course, been other "cure-all" technologies that flourished during the last few years, technologies such as relational databases, 4GLs, and expert systems that were each supposed to solve the software crisis of its day. Just as those technologies failed to solve all of the problems facing them, object technology will fail to solve every problem that IS faces today. Object technology, however, represents a major watershed in the history of computing; it represents a comprehensive change in the way computing systems are organized and it will result in very significant savings. The best way of illustrating the fundamental nature and power of object technology is simply to point out that it will change every important aspect of computing. By the end of the 1990s, companies will be using object-oriented (OO) operating systems and object-oriented client-server networks. They will be developing new applications with object-oriented languages, object-oriented 4GL products, and OO CASE tools, and they will be storing their data in OO databases.

The key to understanding the power of object technology is to think in terms of the underlying infrastructure that all computing systems rely on. Today that infrastructure is based on procedural techniques and those techniques have been pushed to the limits of their power and their flexibility. They have become the problem and not the solution. Object technology will gradually replace procedural techniques and form the new infrastructure of computing. This, in turn, will allow developers and users to attain the computing power and the efficiency they require to solve the business problems of the 1990s.

THE RANGE OF OBJECT-BASED PRODUCTS AND SERVICES

In the first chapter we reviewed the basic concepts of object technology. In this chapter we consider how object technology will be packaged for commercial use. In other words, we consider how a company might acquire the object-based systems and tools to install the object infrastructure it will need to succeed in the 1990s.

Exhibit 2.1 provides an overview of the general types of products in the OO market, as well as some of their major competitors.

The four key product groups in the OT market are (1) operating systems, (2) databases, (3) development tools, and a unique new product category: (4) class libraries. In addition, there are OO network managers (client-server architectures)

Exhibit 2.1   Niches for object-oriented products and their competitors.

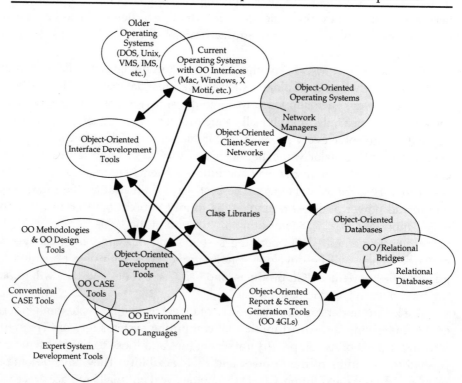

that will ultimately be part of OO operating systems and serve as the conduit for messages between everything else. There are also OO interface development tools that allow developers to create OO interfaces for existing operating systems. (Since existing operating systems are not truly OO and do not include class libraries, these tools make it much easier for a developer to create a good interface in Windows, Motif, etc.) In addition, there are 4GL-like OO tools that allow developers or end users to develop screen or report applications that rely on existing relational databases or on OO databases.

There are also products that help developers create OO applications. This general category includes a number of different types of products, including conventional CASE tools (these develop mainframe applications in COBOL, although they are rapidly moving to other hardware and trying to add C/C++), technical CASE tools that run on Unix workstations and are very interested in adding OO capabilities, as well as products that are especially designed to facilitate the development of OO applications. All OO development tools depend on one or several OO methodologies, which manifest themselves in the diagrams used to analyze and design applications.

We consider products in five major areas: class libraries, operating systems and networks, application development tools, databases, and training and consulting products. To emphasize both the power and flexibility of object technology and to remind you of how all of the familiar system components will be given a slightly new cast in the object-based systems of the 1990s, we begin by considering class libraries and then turn to the more conventional software categories.

CLASS LIBRARIES

If object technology and open systems are going to deliver the benefits that everyone hopes for, they must provide two things: (1) reusable code and (2) the ability to mix modules from different vendors to create a tailored solution for your company. When you write an application in COBOL you write all the application code in COBOL. When you write an application in C++ or Smalltalk, on the other hand, you write some of the code in C++ or Smalltalk, but you get most of the code by using pre-existing classes. Collections of pre-existing classes are typically called *class libraries* or *frameworks*. (Frameworks are just larger collections of classes.) Independent vendors are currently entering the software market to sell class libraries.

Consider a simple example that will illustrate code reuse. In 1992, Texas Instruments (TI) began to use a large, new, fully automated, flexible semiconductor wafer fabrication system that was developed in Smalltalk-80. A quick overview of the code used in TI's system reveals that most of the basic code was provided by language vendors (classes that came with ParcPlace's Smalltalk) or other OO

Exhibit 2.2   Code developed for Texas Instrument's C/M project.

	Classes	Methods
Code developed from scratch (or via subclassing)	1040	20100
Code taken from other products	1550	28900

vendors who provided libraries of classes that encapsulated specialized functionality (see Exhibit 2.2). In some cases the classes provided by the outside vendors were used without modification, but in many cases, TI modified the classes they used by creating subclasses and adding new attributes or new methods to tailor the classes for the specific system TI was creating.

Moreover, since the CIM system that TI developed was the first major OO CIM project undertaken by TI, the developers were forced to create many specific classes from scratch. TI developed most of these new classes with an eye toward reusing these classes in subsequent applications. Whole collections of classes (frameworks) were created in such a way that they could be used in future applications, either directly, or after they had been specialized via subclassing. A good example was the Smidgits framework that TI designed to facilitate tailoring end-user interfaces. TI expects to reuse the Smidgits framework in many subsequent applications. Meanwhile, ParcPlace is offering a commercial version of Smidgits, called VisualWorks. It is easy to imagine that if TI set out to create a new process control application for another wafer fabrication facility, they might be able to reuse more than two-thirds of the code from their current application. This would mean that the new development team would end up writing only about one-third of the total code involved in that future system.

There has always been some reuse of code, of course, and some companies have sold COBOL code or C libraries for others to use. In general, however, when COBOL or C programmers begin to plan a new application, they never expect to get over half the data structures and more than half the procedural code from pre-existing code libraries. OO programming shifts the task from designing and writing code to deciding what pre-existing classes to use and then creating the new code necessary to tailor and structure the new application. It is a whole new kind of programming, and it is only the beginning.

The TI folks depended on an existing operating system (Unix) to provide all their I/O and systems' services. There is no alternative at the moment. In a few years, however, OO operating systems will be available. OO operating systems will not be products as we know them now; they will be collections of classes or frameworks. Developers as sophisticated as the designers who worked on TI's CIM system will be able to decide which operating system classes they want to use, which they want to subclass and tailor, and which classes to obtain from other sources. TI might, for example, develop its own screen interface (e.g., a specially tailored windows environment that incorporates elements of their Smidgits interface tailoring tools), or use a specialized client-server communication framework that is especially tailored for TI's worldwide computer network. Thus, in the near future, the people designing an application may create applications that use specialized classes drawn from operating systems, other applications, languages, and OODB's. Exhibit 2.3 suggests how a single application of the future will be composed of class libraries and frameworks drawn from many sources.

Exhibit 2.3 hardly captures the full complexity of applications that will be built in the near future, but it certainly suggests some of it. Applications themselves will lose their distinctive borders as they draw on classes from libraries provided by multiple operating system frameworks, various language vendors, and other specialized class library vendors, and from libraries that the company develops in the process of creating internal applications. The heart of an application will be the dynamic and persistent instances used when the application is actually run. When one thinks about the code that makes up the application or about maintenance issues, one will be forced to think of all of the classes that are drawn on for the creation of the instances that are used when an application is being run.

Exhibit 2.3   An application comprised of classes drawn from many sources.

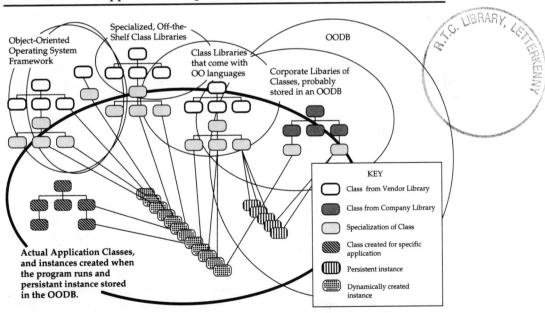

There are two keys to class library-based software development. First, professionally developed class libraries must be available. Second, some system must be available to serve as a buffer between the various class libraries and the applications that want to use them.

There are, already, a number of class libraries for sale. In general there are two broad categories of class libraries: (1) class libraries that help with very fine-grained aspects of program development and (2) class libraries that provide domain-specific functionality. The former are being sold by the language vendors and by class library vendors who are focused on such things as interface design. The class libraries provided by ParcPlace with their Smalltalk products and specialized classes available from vendors such as Code Farms and ObjectGraphics for C++ development are good examples of the former. Libraries providing domain-specific functionality will be sold by specialized consulting companies or by corporations themselves. Thus, companies that formerly sold insurance accounting software will soon also be offering frameworks and class libraries for insurance applications. Similarly, TI has already announced that they might make some of their CIM frameworks available in the future.

Having mentioned some professionally developed class libraries and frameworks, we should hasten to add that the whole field of class library products is just beginning, and, in general, is not ready for general use. It is not that some of the individual class libraries do not work very well. Class libraries are not ready for general commercial use because they are all language or product specific. MacApp is OK for Macintosh applications, but it doesn't help if you are developing an application and want it to run on both a Mac and in Windows 3.0. Similarly, the classes in ParcPlace's Smalltalk work very well as long as you write your entire application in Smalltalk, but they are no help if you want to write your application in C++. Before a corporation begins to assemble class libraries for application development, it needs to be assured that all the classes it acquires or creates can be used in any future applications it decides to develop.

Any large company will want to create some fine-grained applications in a language like C++, some user-friendly applications in a language like Smalltalk, and some CASE-based applications in OO CASE tools as well as a number of other applications in products like HyperCard and PowerBuilder. To really begin to take advantage of the OO revolution, a corporation needs to be assured that all the classes it buys or develops can be used in future applications.

You might think the easy solution to this problem would be to select an OODB and store all your company's classes in that OODB. There are two problems with that approach. First, OODBs are written in specific languages. Thus an OODB written in an extended version of C++ may not store Smalltalk objects, let alone Tool Book or Hypercard objects. In addition, OODBs are proprietary, and they are not mature enough to support a company-wide library of classes. OODBs may be the answer of the future, but they are not the answer for companies that want to begin making a serious commitment to OO development in 1993.

The second approach is to have some intermediate system that can translate objects from one language to another. In effect, the Object Management Group's common object request broker architecture (CORBA) provides a standardized syntax that would facilitate that process if the developers of various class libraries, language compilers, and OODBs all support it. Most OO vendors have announced their intention to support CORBA. In addition, several companies are working on implementations of CORBA that will be included in operating systems.

Most of the applications we consider in this book made use of class libraries provided by the language vendors if they used object-oriented languages and, in many cases, they used specialized class libraries for screen interface development. In general, however, the applications in this book illustrate only a rudimentary use of class libraries. We expect the use of class libraries to grow rapidly in the next few years as more companies learn about object technology and as class libraries and CORBA become more common.

OBJECT-ORIENTED OPERATING SYSTEMS

An object-oriented operating system is designed so that users can take advantage of objects as they use the operating system. An object-oriented operating system does not have to be written in an object-oriented language. An operating system can simply add an OO interface to hide the procedural core. In the long run, however, this won't provide the power and flexibility of a pure OO operating system. In a pure OO operating system, the entire operating system is derived from one or a few highly abstract classes by means of inheritance. This, in turn, means that the structure and function of the operating system can be modified by the developer or user to handle new problems as they arise.

Current windows-based operating systems are best described as object-enhanced. They have put a layer of object technology on top of an underlying procedural structure. There is no sense in which one can examine the classes or subclass of the basic structures in any of the current crop of operating systems (see Exhibit 2.4). The only OO operating system that we know of is GO's PenPoint operating system. The only full-scale OO operating system that has been announced is Taligent's OO operating system.

Pure OO languages, such as Smalltalk, have a root object from which everything else in the language inherits. In effect, the root object tells all of the other objects what it means to be an object. OO languages such as C++ are essentially defined by a core of procedural code to which objects have been added as an additional data type. In either case, there is some kernel of code that establishes the basic nature of the system. In an OO operating system this kernel will probably function like a root object in Smalltalk, but it may very well contain a lot more code than the Smalltalk kernel contains. Efficiency issues may demand that the kernel include procedural code to perform some core functions. In any case, other

Exhibit 2.4   Operating systems.

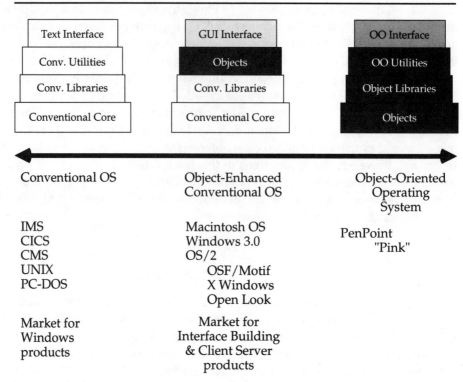

Text Interface	GUI Interface	OO Interface
Conv. Utilities	Objects	OO Utilities
Conv. Libraries	Conv. Libraries	Object Libraries
Conventional Core	Conventional Core	Objects

Conventional OS	Object-Enhanced Conventional OS	Object-Oriented Operating System
IMS	Macintosh OS	PenPoint
CICS	Windows 3.0	"Pink"
CMS	OS/2	
UNIX	OSF/Motif	
PC-DOS	X Windows	
	Open Look	
Market for Windows products	Market for Interface Building & Client Server products	

parts of the operating system will probably be composed of modules of classes that inherit their basic structure and functionality from the kernel. For security reasons, the kernel will probably not be open for modification, although most if not all of the modules that inherit from the kernel should be open to developers who need to specialize or modify them for special purposes.

True OO operating systems will probably eliminate the need for interface building products like ImageSoft's CommonViews, Borland's' Windows LLD, and Apple's MacApp. The developer who uses a true OO operating system should be able to do interface development within the operating system itself by modifying the classes that control the interface that are provided as an integral part of the operating system. (Of course, since OO operating systems are flexible, users may choose to use a core OO operating system and then use an interface framework from another vendor.)

A subtler issue involves the OO functionality of the interface itself. The OO metaphor suggests that we should be able to manipulate objects on the screen. Macintosh OS and NeXTSTEP go one step in this direction by providing trash cans and black holes. In either case, when the user is done with a file, he or she simply drags the file to the trash can and gets rid of it. New Wave, an overlay that makes other operating systems more object oriented, allows users to open applications by simply dragging a file to a program. In effect, you put the file into the program and the program opens the file. There is a limit to how far the OO metaphor can be carried, but expect a real object-oriented operating system to take it a good bit further than any of the current operating systems have to date.

A full-scale OO operating system will need to manage communications between other computers and databases. In effect, each computer (client or server or both) will be an "object" in a client-server network. The objects in the network will communicate by means of messages. To assure that it happens efficiently, vendors of hardware and software must agree on a common syntax for messages. There are a number of network management products, but no existing operating system is capable of independently managing OO-based communications within a client-server network. Exhibit 2.5 provides an overview of an idealized OO operating system with some frameworks.

No full-scale operating system for a conventional computer is entirely written in an OO language. NeXTSTEP has a significant part written in Objective C. New

Exhibit 2.5   An idealized object-oriented operating system.

THE NETWORK OF CLIENTS, AND SERVERS

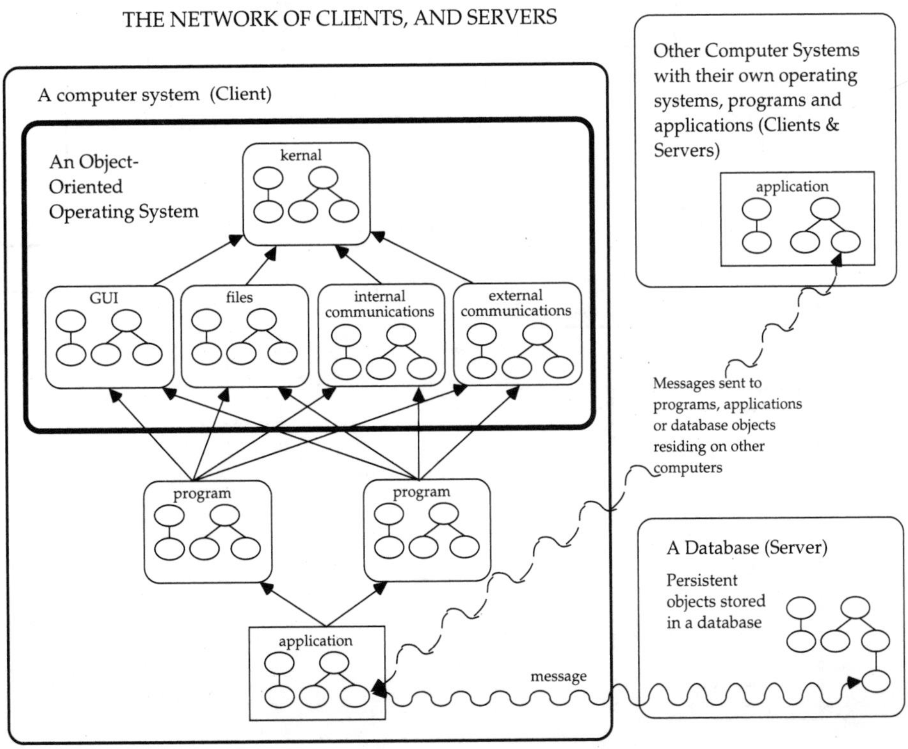

Wave is written in C but incorporates an OO architecture and may be rewritten in C++. Apple and IBM have proposed to develop jointly the first true OO operating system, but that is at least a couple of years off. (Microsoft is also rumored to be working on an OO operating system to follow NT.) At the moment all of the interface development frameworks are limited because they sit on top of operating systems that are not, themselves, object oriented.

GO's PenPoint operating system for its handwriting-based computer is the only true object-oriented operating system that we know of at the moment. The classes that make up the operating system are divided into frameworks. Each framework is responsible for a specific type of functionality. Thus, for example, when a developer wants to create a new application, he or she creates an instance of classes in the application framework and gets the overall screen with its various windows and icons (see Exhibit 2.6).

Exhibit 2.6   The PenPoint class library and an application.

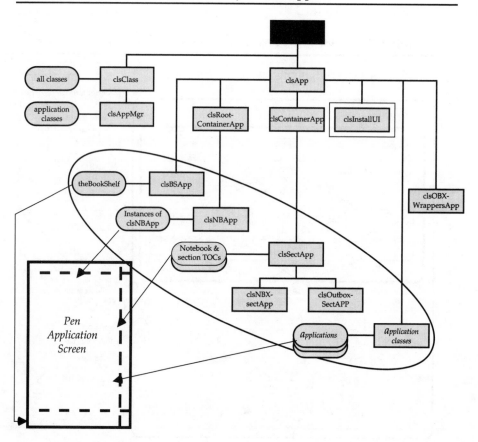

PenPoint, however, is designed to run on specialized hardware, not in client-server environments. Thus, although PenPoint is interesting, it's only a limited example of the full-scale OO operating systems that we will begin to see by the mid-1990s. While we wait for true OO operating systems, a number of products are being marketed to enhance existing windows-based operating systems.

INTERFACE DEVELOPMENT TOOLS

Interface development tools are highly specialized. They provide class libraries and graphical and editing facilities that make it easy for a developer to create an interface for a specific operating system. The best of the interface tools allow the developer to create one interface and then move it to several different operating systems.

Some of the better-known interface tools include Action!, CommonView 2, Object/1, VisualWorks, and WindowBuilder. In effect, an interface tool provides a screen development environment and class libraries for one or more of the common graphical operating systems (e.g., Windows 3, Presentation Manager, New Wave, OSF/Motif, Mac).

Several other tools, including OO development tools and 4GL/Screen Generation tools, like PowerBuilder, and expert system tools like KnowledgePro, are often described as interface development tools because people focus on their graphical capabilities and the fact that they can be used to create interfaces. These tools can be used to develop interfaces, but they can also be used to develop some or all of the application that lies behind the interface and should more properly be classified differently.

APPLICATION DEVELOPMENT LANGUAGES AND TOOLS

One sign that OO adoptions at Fortune 500 companies are still in the early stages is the emphasis on OO languages. When broader adoptions pick up speed, most companies will probably move away from languages to application development tools of various kinds. It is a lot easier to train a COBOL programmer to use an OO 4GL or an OO CASE tool than C++ or Smalltalk. Besides, tools offer the developer the best of both worlds. The programmer can work in a user-friendly development environment that provides the flexibility of interpreted Smalltalk and then let the tool compile the resulting application into a more efficient langauge like C or C++ for runtime execution. One way to think of the options open to corporate developers is to think of layers of software, with Assembler on the bottom, higher level languages above that, CASE tools on top of that, and applications on the top. Another way to conceptualize the same thing is to think of a continuum that runs from languages on the left side to finished appli-

Exhibit 2.7   The language–application continuum.

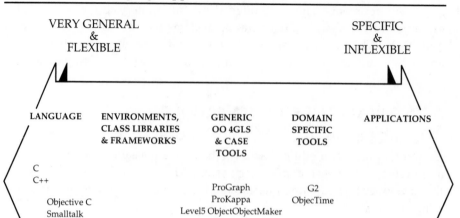

cations on the right side (see Exhibit 2.7). On the left side of the continuum are languages, like C++ and Smalltalk. Languages are very general and completely flexible: you can write anything in a language. To build a very complex application in a language, however, is a demanding task. It takes a lot of time to master a language. Most conventional languages are, in fact, syntactic conventions and a compiler. The syntax of the language determines how you express yourself in the language while the compiler turns your source code into compiled binary code.

Some languages offer more. Interpreted languages allow the developer to write code and then execute the code. Thus, in CenterLine's C++ environment or Digitalk's Smalltalk V, the developer can create and test a program to be sure that it does what is expected before it is compiled. Incremental compilation falls somewhere between a real interpreted language and a compiled language in terms of ease of use. Interpreted languages and incrementally compiled languages both make application development much easier, especially if one is using a rapid prototyping methodology.

Most object-oriented languages (OOLs) also provide class libraries. Each class encapsulates some functionality. Thus, ObjectWorks/Smalltalk, from ParcPlace includes the Smalltalk interpreter, plus an extensive class library, plus utilities for browsing and executing code. Most products provided by OOL vendors, in contrast to the packages provided by conventional language dealers (typically a reference manual and a compiler), fall in the environment category. One still creates an application by writing code, but one has much more support, and class libraries provide code that has already been written.

We place tools in the middle of the continuum. A tool provides a much more complex environment in which to create an application. CASE tools allow the developer to create an application by diagramming the application via some set of symbols (entity diagrams, flow charts, etc.). Some of the 4GL tools allow the user to use visual programming techniques to create an application. Others allow the developer to create graphical user interfaces using icons from pallets of already-drawn icons. If the tool is appropriate to the task the developer addressing it will generally make development faster. There is less code to write and many details will be handled by the tool. On the other hand, trying to use a tool to accomplish a task for which it is not appropriate can be very frustrating. Tools are generally less flexible than languages. The things built into the tool to make it faster in some cases, become obstacles to get around in others.

Further along the continuum are domain and problem-specific tools—expert system-building tools, CAD/CAM tools, case-based reasoning tools, tools for creating airline scheduling applications, spreadsheet tools. The power and the limitations of these tools is even more pronounced. Who would want to write a spreadsheet application in a language when you could just buy a product such as Excel and create your spreadsheet in the course of an afternoon? On the other hand, you would not want to try to create a CIM application in a spreadsheet. As tools become more specialized they assume more about the nature of the resulting application, provide more built-in features, utilities and class libraries, and constrain the developer to a greater degree.

On the extreme right of the continuum we have applications. Companies are buying more and more off-the-shelf applications and end users, of course, normally use applications. An application is specific and inflexible. It does what it is designed to do. There is either a nearly perfect match between the end user's task and the application, or it is useless.

One way or another, everything to the right of languages on the continuum must be compiled into binary code before it can be run on a computer. As you go right on the continuum, you increase the level of abstraction at which you work. An application is very specific in the sense that it deals with a concrete task. It is very abstract in the sense that a user can run the application without knowing anything about how a computer functions. Tools lying in the middle are a lot more abstract than languages. You normally work with diagrams rather than code. They are usually more constrained than languages, but they offer the developer lots of code that he or she does not need to recreate.

We consider two general points along the language–tool–application continuum: (1) languages and environments, and (2) OO tools of various kinds. We do not consider applications here. The remainder of the book is devoted to the consideration of various OO applications.

OBJECT-ORIENTED LANGUAGES AND ENVIRONMENTS

Object-oriented applications can be written in either conventional or object-oriented languages, but they are much easier to write in languages that are especially designed for OO programming. If we were to classify languages according to their OO capabilities, we would get a continuum that looks like the one in Exhibit 2.8.

OO language experts sometimes divide OO languages into two categories, *hybrid languages* and *pure OO languages*. Hybrid languages are languages based on some non-OO model that has been enhanced by OO concepts. Pure OO languages, on the other hand, are entirely based on OO principles. A pure OO language is based on a root or top object and everything else in the language is derived (subclassed) from the root object. Both C++ and CLOS are hybrid languages.

C++ is a superset of C and CLOS is an object-enhanced version of Lisp. Smalltalk, Simula, Eiffel, and a few other languages are pure OO languages. At the moment, the most popular OO language for commercial use is C++. The advantage of C++ is its syntactical familiarity—it is very much like C, and many programmers already know C. In addition, C++ contains many features that make it relatively efficient when it is executed. The disadvantages are two-fold. First, because it's like C, many programmers read about C++, think they understand OO programming, and proceed to write code that lacks any of the advantages one expects from good OO code. Second, although C++ supports all of the

Exhibit 2.8   The power and flexibility of various languages.

The Power and Flexibility of Languages

Low Power; Inflexible   Powerful; Very Flexible

<-->

Conventional Procedural Languages	Object-Based Languages	Minimal OO Languages	Pure OO Languages	Advanced OO Languages
No OO Features	Classes & Instances but no Hierarchical inheritance or message passing	All basic features but with limited polymorphism and dynamics	All basic features and with good polymorphism and dynamics	All basic features and with extraordinary polymorphism and dynamics
COBOL, Fortran PL/1 Pascal C	Ada	C++ Object Pascal	Smalltalk Objective C Eiffel	CLOS Object Prolog

basic OO features, it is a strongly typed language and lacks the extensive poly-morphism, the dynamics, and the memory management features that many OO programmers expect. It is easy to understand why so many companies have embraced C++ for their OO development efforts, but it is really a lot easier to write good OO programs in a pure OO language like Smalltalk or Eiffel.

The major alternative to C++ is Smalltalk. Smalltalk is the most popular pure OO language, and it was the first widely used OO language. The advantages of Smalltalk are its consistency and its flexibility. Smalltalk enforces encapsulation, for example, and provides garbage collection. It makes it easy to write good OO applications and especially easy to write graphical applications. An increasing number of high-end OO applications are being developed in Smalltalk.

The disadvantages of Smalltalk are two-fold. First, Smalltalk is not a well-known language. To use it programmers must learn a new syntax and, more important, they must really learn OO design and development. Second, Smalltalk is generally perceived as more difficult to integrate with existing systems, and its dynamics can make it run slower than C++. Both of these problems are being successfully addressed, although it is too early to dismiss them entirely. There are other pure OO languages (e.g., Eiffel, which is popular in Europe), but they share Smalltalk's problems and are less popular than Smalltalk.

CLOS, an object-enhanced version of Lisp, is a very powerful and flexible language that is popular in universities; its use will probably be confined to universities, aerospace, and other high-tech companies. In addition, it will be used to develop OO CASE and 4GL tools and other very powerful products.

We expect that most corporations will end up using both languages, C++ for more conventional applications and applications where speed is of the essence; Smalltalk for more complex and interface-intensive applications.

In the long run, however, we do not expect that corporations will develop most of their OO applications in either C++ or Smalltalk; we expect them to develop their applications in 4GL or CASE-like tools that will combine the best features of both languages.

Most managers who have thought about OO realize that the major obstacles to introducing OO techniques in the typical Fortune 500 company are cultural and educational in nature, not technical. The people who currently develop applications have to be induced to abandon what they have been doing and begin anew. Moving from COBOL to C++ or Smalltalk is not easy. Even if a programmer learns the basics of C++, he or she often just uses C++ to write bad COBOL applications. If the OO revolution is to be successful, developers will have to learn a whole new way of conceptualizing application development and new OO methodologies. It is probably easier to switch methodologies if you move from COBOL to an OO CASE tool where you diagram the application, since the tool tends to enforce an OO structure.

Many arguments between the C++ and the Smalltalk people can be resolved by using tools. Most tools are made up of two parts: a development environment and a runtime environment. The development environment can be interpreted and dynamic. It can provide memory management and all kinds of browsers. In effect, the development environment can be like Smalltalk. When the developer is satisfied with the application, it can be converted to code for execution. The code generated by the tool can be more efficient, more like C++ or C than Smalltalk. A tool allows the developer to avoid having to choose between ease of development and efficient execution.

Then there are the legacy applications that every company is trying to maintain. For many, a tool that facilitates both OO development and still provides support for existing applications (e.g., some kind of encapsulation facilities for COBOL or, better yet, re-engineering facilities) seems like the best of both worlds.

4GL AND CASE PRODUCTS

Having considered OO languages, we now consider the tools that one finds in the OO market at the moment. The obvious categories include:

- Upper CASE products (analysis and design tools)

- Application Generators (code generators, OO 4GLs, interface generators)

- OO I-CASE products (integrated sets of Upper and Lower CASE tools)

- Domain-specific CASE products (tools for developing specific types of applications)

- OO Meta-CASE Products (tools for developing CASE products)

Miscellaneous OO Life Cycle Management Tools

Exhibit 2.9 provides one way of thinking about these products. We have compared the products to a very simplified version of the OO software life cycle. The OO life cycle is not as linear as conventional development, and we have shown analysis, design, and programming overlapping to suggest the spiral development pattern that is typical of this phase of the development process. (In fact, when one considers the effects of class reuse, the OO life cycle can look much different from the one we have shown in Exhibit 2.9.) In spite of the differences, the OO tools can, in general, be analyzed according to the same categories one uses with conventional CASE tools.

Exhibit 2.9 OO 4GL and CASE products.

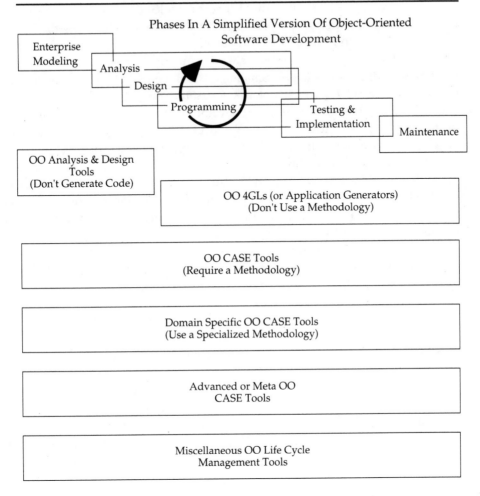

OO Upper CASE Products (Analysis and Design Tools)

Just as there are conventional Upper CASE products, there are OO Upper CASE products—OO analysis and design tools that automate various OO methodologies.

The conventional CASE arena is dominated by structured methodologies, and especially by James Martin's Information Engineering methodology (implemented by Texas Instrument's IEF and KnowledgeWare's ADW, two dominant I-CASE vendors). There is no similar consensus in the OO arena; instead there are a variety of OO methodologies. No OO methodology really covers the entire software life cycle in the way the latest structured methodologies do, nor are the OO methodologies very mature. When you consider that the structured methodologies were all designed to facilitate COBOL development, and only recently enhanced for C development, it makes sense that new methodologies designed to handle languages as different as C++, Smalltalk, Eiffel, and CLOS might not agree on even the basics of OO development. Issues that the conventional CASE tools never had to face, like those involving spiral development, dynamic methods, and interpreted development tools, make a good OO methodology much harder to develop. No current OO methodologies really handle the use of class libraries or provide much help in creating classes for reuse. In addition, while some methodologists want to focus entirely on OO development and ignore procedural systems, others want to develop methodologies that function as bridges between procedural methodologies and OO methodologies, and still others want to create methodologies that can encompass both approaches.

The variety and immaturity of OO methodologies is, of course, reflected in the OO analysis and design tools on the market. Most of the tools were developed by a methodologist, or someone working closely with a single methodologist. Some of the more popular A&D tools and methodologies are listed in Exhibit 2.10.

Several methodologies, including Martin/Odell's new OO methodology, Ptech, and Shlaer/Mellor's real-time OO methodology are supported by OO CASE tools that we will consider in a moment. All of the tools are being rapidly enhanced to reflect changes in the underlying methodology and to remain competitive. We expect that in the course of the next two or three years all of the current crop of OO analysis and design tools will either disappear, or they will be enhanced to become OO CASE tools. In other words, OO analysis and design vendors will add code generation to their Upper CASE offering and move into the integrated OO CASE arena.

Exhibit 2.10   OO tools and methodologies.

Tool Vendor	Tool	Methodology
Object International	OOATool	Coad/Yourdon's OOA/OOD
Objective Systems	Objectory	Objectory
Ptech	Ptech	Ptech
Rational Inc.	ROSE	Booch's Object Design
General Electric	OMTool	Rumbaugh, et al. Object Modeling
T.N.I.	STOOD	HOOD methodology

OO 4GLs or Application Generators

The term *4GL* really does not mean much in conventional computing, and it means even less when applied to an OO product. Some OO 4GL products are designed to work with relational databases (e.g., ParcPlace's VisualWorks); other OO 4GLs are designed to work with OODBs (Servio's GeODE). More to the point, there are many OO development tools that draw on class libraries, create interfaces, and generate code. If we keep the criteria that we use in the conventional arena—Lower CASE tools and 4GLs do not depend on a methodology, but Upper and Integrated CASE tools do—then most of the OO tools on the market fall into the non-methodology-based, bottom-up category. We will adopt the term *OO Application Development Tools* and use it in contrast to OO Upper and I-CASE products and as a broad synonym for OO 4GLs, OO Lower CASE tools, and various other OO code generators. At least two expert system tool companies have taken to talking about their upcoming products as OO 4GL or application generator products, so we would include them in this category as well.

As with operating systems and languages, one must discriminate between object-enhanced products and true object-oriented products (see Exhibit 2.11). The

Exhibit 2.11   Non-OO, object-enhanced and OO products.

Text Interface	GUI Interface	OO Interface
Conv. Utilities	OO Framework	OO Utilities
Conv. Libraries	Conv. Libraries	Object Libraries
Conventional Core	Conventional Core	OO Framework
Conventional Language	Conventional Language	OO Language

Conventional Products	Object-Enhanced Products	Object-Oriented Products
4GL • Focus • Sybase	• ProGraph • ObjectVision	• ObjectWorks + VisualWorks • GeODE
CASE • IEF • ADW • Oracle CASE	• OO (IDE) • ObjectMaker	

key is the underlying nature of the product. If the product is a true object-oriented tool, it will be written in an object-oriented language. In effect, the tool will be a set of frameworks that the developer can subclass and enhance to suit his or her specific needs. Most of the OO application generators on the market at this time are object-enhanced. The underlying product is written in a langauge like C and object-oriented capabilities have been added on top. Or, even if they are written in an object-oriented langauge, all of the classes comprising the tool are locked so that a developer cannot access them. True OO application generators provide OO developers with lots of flexibility—in a sense they are closer to OO environments. (In another sense, OO application generators are like meta-4GL tools: you can keep modifying the underlying structure of the tool to create different application development tools.) Object-enhanced application generators offer less flexibility, but, for those less familiar or confident, they are certainly easier to learn to use.

Just as we can distinguish among OO languages like C++, Smalltalk, and CLOS, we can classify the current OO application generator products into three subcategories:

- Basic OO Products (Tools that support C++-like functionality; tools, in other words, that offer only a rather limited degree of dynamics and poly-morphism and lack features like dynamic memory allocation.) Some examples include Borland's ObjectVision, Objective's MacroScope, and PowerSoft's PowerBuilder.

- Dynamic OO Products (Tools that support Smalltalk-like functionality; tools that support greater dynamics and memory allocation.) Some examples include TGS Systems' ProGraph, and Serius's Serius Developer.

- Advanced OO Products (Tools that support features found in CLOS—the Common Lisp Object Standard; tools that support frame or slot-like structures; incorporate constraints on attribute inheritance, inferencing, and rules; and dynamic class and attribute generation.) Good examples are Inference's ART Enterprise, IntelliCorp's ProKappa, and Hitachi's Object IQ.

Another key to dividing OO application generators into niches is to consider what type of developer the product is designed for. Some OO application generators are very sophisticated products designed for sophisticated developers. Others are very simple and are designed to make it possible for non-programmers or domain experts to create useful applications. Exhibit 2.12 provides a second way of looking at OO CASE and application development products that puts less emphasis on traditional CASE distinctions and more on the power and flexibility of the tool and on the intended user.

Exhibit 2.12   An overview of OO application development products.

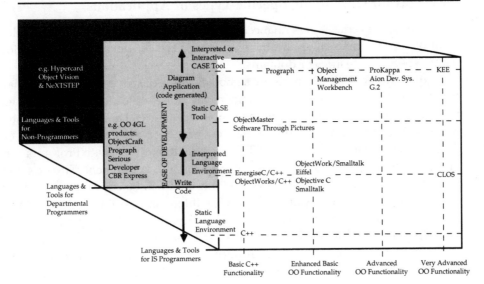

OO I-CASE Products
(Integrated Sets of Upper and Lower CASE tools)

Everything we said about the variety and immaturity of OO methodologies, when we considered OO analysis and design tools, applies as well to I-CASE tools. Similarly, the distinction we just made between object-enhanced and true object-oriented 4GL tools applies to OO CASE tools as well.

Conventional CASE vendors are enhancing their tools to incorporate OO techniques. TI, for example, has announced that Version 6.0 of their popular IEF CASE tool will incorporate a limited OO capability. Technical CASE Vendors (CASE on UNIX platforms that generate Ada or C code) like Cadre Technologies' Teamwork, and IDE's Software Through Pictures have already incorporated OO A&D tools in their products and have announced that their tools will be able to generate C++ in the future. Mark V's ObjectMaker and Popkin's System Architect already support several different OO methodologies and generate Ada and C++ code.

In addition to the conventional CASE vendors, several new companies have entered the I-CASE market and are offering OO CASE tools that rely on OO methodologies and generate conventional or OO languages. Good examples include Ipsys Ltd.'s Ipsys HOOD Toolset, Verilog's Object Editor, ObjecTime's ObjecTime, Mark V Systems' ObjectMaker, IntelliCorp's Object Management Workbench, ProtoSoft's Paradigm Plus, and Ptech's Ptech product.

Problem- or Domain-specific CASE Products
(Tools for Developing Specific Types of Applications)

There are several object-enhanced tools that are specialized for the development of specific kinds of applications or specialized for developing applications within specific industries or domains.

Expert system-building tools are a good example of specialized tools that have significant OO capabilities. At the moment the most sophisticated expert system vendors are working to reposition their tools as either OO application generators or OO CASE tools. The expert systems vendors that have the best story for OO development are Inference, with ART Enterprise, IntelliCorp, with ProKappa, and Trinzic, with Aion, which provides a complete OO environment. Trinzic's Aion tool runs on PCs and mainframes (something that will be critical once corporate IS people really start to pay attention to OT). Inference is selling both ART Enterprise and its case-based reasoning tool, CBR Express (which is object-enhanced) for help desk applications; IntelliCorp is implementing James Martin's new OO CASE methodology on top of their ProKappa tool. Similarly, Information Builders Inc. is integrating their OO expert system product (Level5 Object) with their 4GL offerings.

Several of the CAD/CAM tools on the market rely on OO technology. Similarly, G2, by Gensym, is a very popular OO/AI tool that is primarily used to develop real-time plant simulation and process control systems.

Meta-CASE Products (Tools for Developing CASE Products)

In a very real sense, any true OO CASE tool is a meta-CASE tool. We considered dropping this category, or limiting the OO CASE category to the object-enhanced tools and putting all of the true OO CASE tools in this category. After looking at the products, we decided that we could make some useful distinctions and decided to keep this category. Some OO I-CASE products are really designed for corporate programmers and are designed to support day-to-day application development. A few tools, such as Mark V's ObjectMaker and Ipsys' Toolset product, on the other hand, are really designed to be used to develop other CASE products.

Miscellaneous OO Life Cycle Tools

In addition to the other tools we have mentioned, there are OO equivalents of conventional products to help managers control the software development process. We do not consider these in any detail at the moment, but some are very useful, although most, in the long run, will probably get incorporated into OO CASE products. A good example of a tool in this category is ENVY Developer.

ENVY is designed to work with Smalltalk. It coordinates the work of several developers who are working on a common project by keeping track of successive modifications and versions. Another example is Digitalk's Team Developer.

We have suggested a number of different products that all rely on OO techniques to facilitate the development of OO or conventional applications. At the moment it is easy to subdivide these products into more or less conventional categories. By the late 1990s, however, we expect that most of these distinctions will disappear and all of the various products we have discussed will evolve into a general-purpose OO-based application development product (see Exhibit 2.13). In some ways the product will probably be like a combination 4GL and CASE tool, but, since it will be based on frameworks and depend on class libraries

Exhibit 2.13   The evolution of the OO application development product of the future.

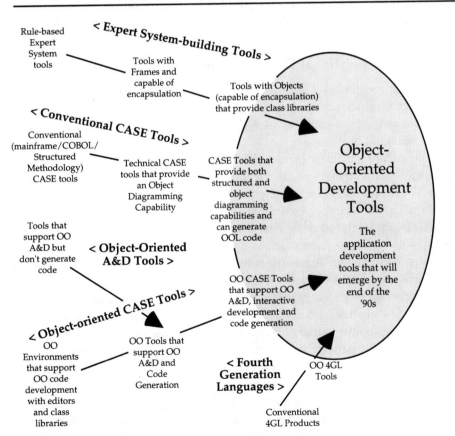

located in the OO operating systems and in OO databases, it will be a much more open product than those we are accustomed to at this time. Most companies will probably use several tools in combination, drawing the frameworks they prefer from each and combining them with frameworks in their operating systems and databases.

Database Products

The use of hierarchical and relational databases have provided organizations with powerful tools to use in organizing application and employee access to data. Existing databases are limited, however. Hierarchical databases are tailored to work with specific programs. Relational databases have provided data independence, but are very limited in the kinds of data types that you can store or manipulate. Relational databases have difficulty with abstract data types, for example, and they cannot handle large structured data items at all. To handle objects and composite objects, relational database management systems must be "extended."

Extended Relational Database Management Systems

There are various ways relational databases can be extended. In general, this is handled by introducing a pre-compiler that takes the structured data items and decomposes them into simpler atomic items that can then be stored in a conventional relational database.

The advantage of the extended relational database approach is that it maintains the relational model that corporations are already using and are familiar with. The disadvantage of the extended approach is that there is significant overhead time involved in pre-compiling structured data to store them and then reassembling the structured data whenever an application needs to use it. Moreover, there is no accepted theory about how to "extend" a relational database, so extended relational databases quickly lose the elegance and simplicity that made the relational model so popular in the first place.

The current extended RDBMS may satisfy the MIS department that wants just to add a few abstract data types or experiment with an application written in C++. They may even satisfy MIS groups that want to introduce a limited version of an Office Information System while keeping everything else much as it is, but they are not nearly ready to handle the needs of serious CAD or CASE users. Ingres and Sybase are good examples of products that are being positioned as extended relational databases. IBM's AD Cycle/Repository is another example of an extended relational database, albeit one specialized to hold CASE information.

Object-Oriented Database Management Systems (OODBMS)

In general, an OODBMS implements object-oriented technology as it has evolved in OOLs like Smalltalk, CLOS, and C + +. In other words, the data model and manipulation language generally resemble one of the current object-oriented languages—although each language must be extended to include a persistent object construct. If the database is based on an object-oriented version of Lisp, it can be quite powerful and can handle all kinds of data types, including strings, objects, and composite objects. If the language is based on Smalltalk, which is a pure object-oriented language, then everything from strings to composite objects must be defined in terms of the object data type. If the language is based on C + +, it can handle a variety of data types but is considerably less flexible, since C + + is essentially a static language, while Lisp and Smalltalk are both interpreted languages that support a number of dynamic operations that cannot be performed in C + +. (C + + OODBs split methods out of the database and place them in separate Unix files, essentially rendering the objects in the database passive.)

The overall architecture of an OODBMS is the same as the RDBMS. The core of each is an environment that is loaded into RAM. This environment handles three general types of things: (1) It provides an interface with developers, with applications that are being run, and with users that want to undertake ad hoc queries; (2) it actually models the data with more or less flexibility and complexity; and (3) it handles the placement and retrieval of data on one or more static storage media. The entire OODBMS runs on a hardware platform within an operating system and is capable of managing distributed databases via a client-server model. To really understand the differences between the functionality of a RDBMS and an OODBMS, or the differences between the various OODBMS products on the market, we need to consider myriad details that are beyond the scope of this chapter.

Some examples of the current OODBs, the languages they were written in, and OO 4GLs sold by the same vendors are included in Exhibit 2.14.

Current OODBs were initially developed to handle single applications, like CAD/CAM systems, and have recently been expanded to handle multiple transactions. There are the same problems with speed and safety that initially plagued the relational databases, and they are being overcome. In addition, OODBs face considerable resistance because many companies have just moved to relational databases and do not even want to think of another major database migration effort. We expect that the move to OODBs will occur only when a company really needs the power and speed that the OODB offers, and that will occur only when companies develop a number of OO applications that rely on complex data types

Exhibit 2.14   Object-oriented databases.

Vendor	OODB	OOL	OO 4GL
Itasca	Itasca	Lisp	
ObjectStore	ObjectDesign	C++	
Ontos, Inc.	Ontos	C++	AD/Tools
Objectivity Inc.	Objectivity	C++	
O2 Technology	O2	C++	
Servio Corp.	Gem Stone	Smalltalk	GeODE
Versant Object Technology Corp.	Versant ODBS	C++	

that will be really hard to handle in either hierarchical or relational databases (e.g., video). During the transition, hierarchical, relational, and OODBs will all co-exist. The OODB vendors are currently adding capabilities that will allow OODBs to communicate with relational databases via SQL and this will facilitate the use of both databases. The move to client-server networks will certainly make it easier to mix databases in the near future. We expect that the ultimate triumph of OO operating systems and large OO applications with their demand for the extensive use of class libraries will eventually push most companies into extensive use of OODBs in the late 1990s.

Object-Oriented Training and Consulting

One final type of OO product ought to be mentioned, simply because this is the type of product that many companies will use as they first introduce object technology to their developers. There is a rapidly growing number of companies that offer training and consulting services designed to help companies learn about object technology and to assist them in their first projects. These companies range from new departments within traditional consulting companies to new startup companies staffed by object-oriented developers. The Object Management Group has made an effort to certify some companies, but there are many good companies that have not applied for certification.

The criteria that apply here are not specific to object technology, but apply to any training or consultancy effort. Obviously the vendor should know the subject matter, but beyond that, they should know how to train or how to assist companies in achieving early successes in this new field. Given the major organizational changes implied by the use of object technology as well as the very significant shift in perspective that object development represents, most companies should certainly give serious thought to a very extensive training effort and consulting support on initial application development efforts.

SUMMARY

Most of this book focuses on applications developed by corporations that are just beginning to explore object technology. It is impressive how much these companies have been able to do with the technology. It is even more impressive when you consider that they have used only the early tools provided by the technology: object-oriented languages, class libraries, and a small set of OO tools.

The interest in objects is driving a rapid expansion of object-oriented products. In the course of the next few years a wide variety of additional OO products will become available to make object-oriented development much more extensive and more effective. More important, the tools will gradually evolve to differ from the current conventional or early OO tools because they will eventually be designed to fit within a very different computing environment where the entire infrastructure will be object-oriented.

As you read the application stories that follow, keep two things in mind. First, these applications are now being used. That means they were developed with products that were available two or three years ago. If the same projects were being done today the developers might choose different languages or tools to work with. Similarly, these are early projects done by individuals that have had to work to convince their companies to try a new technology. Second, individuals that develop new applications in new technologies often become enthusiastic about the particular approach they use. We have tried to leave the enthusiasm in the articles, but we want to warn the reader that someone else might be equally enthusiastic about some other language or tool. The success of these applications should not be taken as an endorsement of particular approaches or products. The products available for OO developers are growing and being improved very rapidly. The products used in the applications reported in this book worked, but different approaches and other tools might be even more effective in 1993.

Domain: Manufacturing

O f the various industry segments, manufacturing has some particularly demanding characteristics for software applications:

- Manufactured products are described by complex, nested information
- Manufacturing processes are typically complex and deeply nested
- Many similar parts and operations must be scheduled and coordinated
- All this complexity must be dealt with in real time with minimal errors

Objects are well suited to meet these demands. The encapsulation of data and process within objects simplifies the relationships between manufacturing materials and their operations. Further, the composition relationship is ideal for handling complex nested structures, and object technology's simulation capabilities are ideal for coordinating the actions of many independent operations.

It should come as no surprise, therefore, that some of the more innovative applications of objects are coming out of the manufacturing arena. The applications presented here are typical: Demanding problems were tackled and solved while also realizing dramatic increases in development productivity and software quality.

In fact, Wacker Siltronic's application provides one of the most compelling demonstrations of increased productivity and quality ever published. When the company set out to automate the scheduling and programming of its silicon furnaces, it took as its model the most modern view of quality management. Its goal was to create a software system with zero defects. It would do this by using a software development system modeled after the red cords on manufacturing lines. If a software defect was ever encountered, the development process would be shut down and the team would work together to fix the process so that type of defect never occurred again.

The result? Over 20,000 lines of code were produced in less than 100 staff days at a cost of only $2 per line. For all this productivity, there were only eight defects detected during the entire development process, and no further defects have been discovered in over two years of continuous use. When was the last time you saw a major system come on line immediately and run defect free for two years?

Another striking thing about the applications described here is that all four yielded significant improvements in the manufacturing process itself. These results indicate that the "second wave" of benefits described in Chapter 1—those accruing to the users rather than the developers—is truly on the rise. Wacker, for example, found that its furnace schedulers now spend only 5% of their time doing scheduling with the new system, a task that used to take nearly all of their time. The application also improved the manufacturing process, saving tens of thousands of dollars per year. According to Wacker's calculations, their system paid for itself in a matter of months.

Boeing Aircraft has enjoyed similar benefits. Its Product Knowledge Manager manages the generation of product documents that used to require up to 40 hours to prepare by hand. With the new system, preparation time averages less than 3 hours and is often complete within 30 minutes. Its new wirewrap system has yielded similar savings: the time to rework a board has been reduced by a factor of five, and errors introduced by engineering change orders were reduced from 10% to less than 1%.

Alumax expects to realize a less dramatic return, at least in terms of percentages. Its new smelter-planning system is expected to reduce the cost of building a new smelter by about 1%. Given that a smelter costs about $1 billion, however, that 1% translates into a savings of $10 million. This means that their new system will pay for itself—including all software and hardware costs—twenty times over the first time it is used.

CHAPTER 3

Application Description

SMELTER INFORMATION SYSTEM

Alumax Primary Aluminum Corporation of Norcross, Georgia is the third largest producer of aluminum in the United States. It builds, owns and operates smelters which process alumina into solid aluminum ingots. Building an aluminum smelter is a major undertaking, currently costing approximately $1 billion.

STATEMENT OF THE PROBLEM

Planning the construction of an aluminum smelter requires input from numerous sources. The information and know-how to build smelters exists within Alumax but is dispersed among many individuals and their filing systems. Jack Judson cites the following specific problems in planning the construction of a new smelter.

- The information was available but not in any usable, organized manner.
- There was no central repository of information.
- The company was dependent on individuals' memories and their information files.
- There was the danger of loss of vital data due to personnel changes and losses.
- Because individual experts were widely dispersed, timely access to information was a problem.
- Difficulty in projecting costs due to geographic, economic, environmental, and cultural factors.
- Difficulty understanding the availability of alternative resources of raw materials worldwide.
- Difficulty in locating and contacting potential equipment suppliers and contractors for specific purposes.

SOLUTION: SMELTER INFORMATION SYSTEM

The Smelter Information System (SIS) provides information for construction, technology and procurement and operations for smelters on a worldwide basis. The system consists of 108 objects at this time and as the system grows, more objects will be added. Approximately 50 methods have been written for auto-inheritance. Of all the methods written, approximately 40% are inherited. Functions, windows, forms and methods in object root can be inherited by all the applications and their objects. Functions, windows, forms and methods in application root can be inherited by objects specific to that application. Text Iform (input form), help, print, screen print functions related to objects, instances, and data elements are provided at the application level, so that the developer does not have to worry about them.

SIS was developed using ODDESY by Lohara Software Systems Inc., an integrated application development tool set using object-oriented methodologies with an interface to a relational database. The interface to relational databases was critical for compatibility with other applications using relational databases. SIS was implemented in a distributed environment, where the UNIX based servers reside in different geographical locations.

Exhibit 3.1   System components.

	Hardware	Software
Interface	IBM RS-6000 Compaq PC 486/50	AIX SCO UNIX/ODT
Core Code		C and 4/5GL ODDESY
Database		Informix
Development Environment	PC 486	ODDESY

Exhibit 3.1 shows the main components of SIS. The application operates in a distributed environment as well as in a client-server mode over LAN and WAN. TCP/IP and X.25 XPC protocols are used for LAN and WAN respectively. Other protocols can be added as the application is communications and database independent.

The application consists of nine major modules and many submodules as follows:

1. Smelter Information
   This module contains six submodules:
   a. Smelter Details: provides key attributes of smelter.
   b. General and Technology Information: By facility and department with interface to hypermedia.
   c. Construction Costs: Total plant costs by area, by facility, by department and by key cost categories. Construction factors by plant wide, by facility, details, text, vendors, and bidders.
   d. Equipment cost by facility, by equipment, by vendor, by bidder including installation materials, labor, civil and other categories.
   e. Major plant contracts by facility, details, text, vendors, and bidders.
   f. Raw materials, requirements, specifications, transport mode, supplier information and historical information. Escalation factors by year, currency factors, are automatically applied depending upon base year and computed year. A complete comparative analysis between smelters is provided for user to evaluate alternatives. Text information or scanned information and help is provided for each data element, object level and data element level.

2. Operational Information
   This module is built by the user. The user can add new data elements from a directory or add the new elements to the directory. If new elements are added to an object, the system automatically generates new methods and links them properly. It is totally driven by the user and no programming changes are needed. Submodules include up to three levels of information for aluminum production, production statistics, electrical power, utilities, raw materials, operating categories, operating costs and financial. The system also allows the option to display with years across (column) or years down (rows).

3. Aluminum Technology
   This module manages the various types of technologies used in smelter operations including comparative analysis factors, and approximate costs. Some of the technologies used are: reduction, anode production, bake oven, rodding, fume treatment, cast house, bath processing, and general information on other processes.

4. Primary Aluminum Production
   Manages primary aluminum production worldwide, by product type and by smelter.

5. Global Materials
   Manages the production and consumption of raw materials on a global basis. Provides information on producers and their suppliers and consum-

ers. Includes such information as supplier details, specifications, transportation and costs, history of supplier and consumer, process parameter related to quality requirements.

6. Global Power

   Manages the availability of power on a country-by-country basis. Type of power, hydro, thermal, nuclear, profile of the utility. Long term production and consumption forecasts.

7. Vendor Profile

   Manages all vendor information.

8. System Directories

   Includes directories for raw materials, owners, equipment, escalation factors, source raw materials, source suppliers, cost categories, construction factors, system parameters, technology parameters, operational information data elements. New directories can be easily built.

9. Query/Report

   Allows the user to run ADHOC Query and report as well as update, delete, modify and print the output. Joins across objects can also be made.

Operations such as new, view, print, modify, delete, details, setup, search pattern, executive view are provided throughout. Global commands such as end input, exit, go to action bar, text, help, interface to hypermedia (text and image) are provided throughout the system. Help is provided for each data element. Form designer and report designer are also provided in an interactive or editor mode. Control A function immediately provides the information about object name, method name, object ID, line number, form name, and window name during execution.

SIS employs the following OO features:

BASIC OO FUNCTIONALITY
   – Classes/Instances.
   – Inheritance/specialization.
   – Methods/messages.

ADVANCED OO FUNCTIONALITY
   – Dynamic class/method generation.

EXTENDED PROGRAMMING ENVIRONMENT
   – Functional programming.

DEVELOPMENT ENVIRONMENT
   – Interpreted internal language
   – Automatic links to databases.

- Editors, indexers, consistency checkers.
- Graphical tool for imaging interface.

STORAGE MANAGEMENT
- Repository available.

CODE GENERATION
- Language code generated. (C)

PROJECT LIFE CYCLE

The development team included Jack Judson, Chief Engineer at Alumax, as well as personnel at Lohara Software Systems of Simi Valley, California.

Analysis and Design

Since this was their first venture into OO, developers decided that an evolutionary approach (shown in Exhibit 3.2) would be appropriate, developing the application in small increments and testing each piece thoroughly.

The application modeling phase was totally user-oriented, with no restrictions on the wish lists. The following objectives were promulgated:

Objectives:

- Develop a model that represents the planning process for the construction of a $1 billion plant.

- Allow users to input all the vital logistic and cost information for the construction of the plant.

- Predict the cost of building a new facility.

- Gather and input vital information about plant operations.

- Gather and input information related to global production and consumption of raw materials and electrical power for the production plant.

- Build a repository for changes and enhancements to related technologies.

User Requirements

- Ease and flexibility of data entry.

- Visualization of information-to-facility relationships.

- Ease of information retrieval and reporting.

- Ease of query of information.

- Cost estimates by department or total plant.

- Provide "what-if" functionality.

Exhibit 3.2   Application development cycle.

Application Development Cycle
The Evolutionary Model

A. Application Modeling

B. Application Development

C. Application Implementation and Maintenance

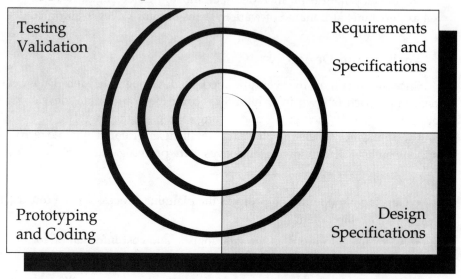

- Provide analytical capability.

- Graphical presentation capability.

- Comparative and competitive information.

- Ability to add to and enhance the system.

Judson describes the modeling process:

First we had to develop an object model. Using the interactive workbench, we started to model the application, designing objects and providing a definition of each object. As we designed, we found that many times we had to move objects as parent/child objects, or combine some into one object. This was where the basic thinking needed change. It was very difficult in the beginning to differentiate between instance/attributes and classes. The system kept us on track and we kept learning as we progressed.

Next we had to develop the application flow of screens and menus. This was done very quickly, in a total of five to seven days. We found it much easier to use paper and pen, or a blackboard to draw the flows and screens. As we built an object, defining the data definition and structure for it, we'd sometimes find that we did not know what data needed to go into it. It would turn out that the object could be represented as attributes of another object.

Subsequently, a designer view has been added to Oddesy which allows the user and the designer to develop application flow, model classes, and define data structures, methods, menus and forms interactively.

Development

The development phase involved four steps which were repeated as the application grew. Most of the work here was done by the system designer and programming staff with input from the user in accepting and testing the prototypes of successive modules.

The four steps of development were:

1. Requirements and specifications provided by the users.

2. Design specifications which were provided by the programming staff and system designer.

3. Prototyping by the programming staff.

4. Test validation by the user, designer, and programming staff.

System requirements developed by the programming staff included:

- Global access.

- Multiple geographical locations.

- Ease of development and maintenance of system.

- Integration of multimedia information.

- Ability to adapt to new technologies.

- Provide interfaces to existing systems, if required.

- Provisions for adaptability to standards and open systems wherever feasible (hardware and software).

- Nine to 12 months for development and implementation.

SIS was developed with ODDESYL, the 4GL language of Oddesy. The language provides standard OO features such as message passing, inheritance, and C language interface. Programming in this phase was done by Lohara Software Systems. Development took one year and required 7,500 person hours.

Exhibit 3.3   SIS Network Topology

Alumax Smelter Information System Network Topology

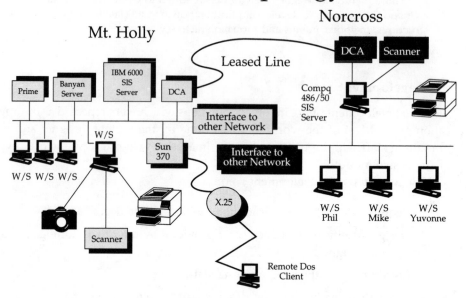

Deployment

The system was installed in a WAN with two server nodes which store the database and client nodes are connected to one of the server nodes. Little effort had to be put into training the user since the users had been actively involved throughout the design and development phase. Likewise, there were no user acceptance issues. Exhibit 3.3 shows the SIS network topology.

Maintenance

A typical requirement in database oriented applications is the ability to change the attributes of various objects. SIS enables users to change the attributes of objects through its setup module. Such changes are automatically propagated to the other network sites, and methods in the affected objects are regenerated to reflect the change. This reduces the maintenance effort to a minimum.

Also, since the application is written in interpreted language, bug fixes and minor enhancements can be carried out by a trained person in the user organization.

BENEFITS

According to Judson,

The system flows very well by using just a few commands. With a few hours of training the users are able to use the system. The system is very intuitive and provides related information automatically. Any number of reports can be generated. Maintenance is minimized and simplified.

I believe that in the construction of our next smelter we can have a savings of 1% or more, which amounts to $10 million or more. The approximate cost of developing and implementing the SIS was less than 5% of the potential savings, including hardware and software.

CONCLUSIONS

In recommending OO to others, Judson lauds OO's spiral methodology:

Savings in development time, implementing changes and adding new modules were substantial. In some cases the changes and additions were made in a matter of hours. From analysis, design, prototyping, unit testing, integration testing and implementation, it was one continuous process and iterations could be made at any level.

Object-oriented technology has certainly lived up to its billing, and I will not hesitate to develop other applications using emerging object-oriented technologies.

CHAPTER 4

Application Description

PRODUCT KNOWLEDGE MANAGER

STATEMENT OF THE PROBLEM

In the mid-1980s magnetics was an area of interest within Boeing. It was determined that the majority of problems originated from a lack of communication between the organizations within the product arena and from inferior product documentation. As a result, products were often built to certain specifications and tested to others. Additionally, documentation generation required in-depth knowledge of the Boeing Drafting Standards as well as documentation generation requirements levied by the program and/or the customer. Only a few specialized engineers and technicians had the breadth and depth of knowledge to correctly generate this documentation.

Boeing attacked the problem in two ways. First, a team approach was implemented to address the communication issues. Second, funding was provided for analysis of the overall product development process; Product Knowledge Manager (PKM) funding was authorized based upon that analysis.

SOLUTION: THE PRODUCT KNOWLEDGE MANAGER

The Product Knowledge Manager (PKM) is a multiphase knowledge based system developed to aid in the life cycle management of Boeing electronic products. Phase I of PKM was placed in production in September, 1987. It provides an intelligent user interface and a documentation facility to generate and manage these documents. The system is written in KEE and LISP. Approximately 60 KEE knowledge bases provide information on products, programs, authorization, drafting standards, and documentation structure. Over 600 LISP functions operate on the knowledge bases to perform user requested operations.

Version 1.00 was released for full production use in October, 1989. This version represented a mature documentation generation, manipulation, and statusing facility.

PKM views documentation production in terms of the overall product life cycle. It provides the user with an intelligent interface to execute analysis and design tools while capturing the product attributes in the appropriate knowledge base. As a side effect of running these applications, required documentation attributes are captured and documentation can be generated semiautomatically. Exhibit 4.1 shows the PKM user interface.

Word processing and documentation generation systems abound within industry. What makes the documentation generation facility of PKM different is how the documentation structure is stored and manipulated. PKM separates the structure of documentation and stores it in an ordered knowledge base, "ordered" meaning that the order of text and graphic sections is fixed unless altered by the user.

Typical documentation consists of title page, revisions page, active sheet record page, table of contents page, text pages, and associated graphics pages. By linking a single parent to each of these components, a structure is formed. In this structure the components become major sections. Each major section in a structure

Exhibit 4.1   PKM system control panel.

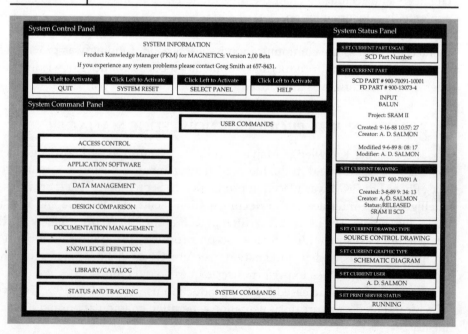

has a Boeing Drafting Standards (BDS) form associated with it. These forms contain formatting constraints as to where, what, and how to place text on them.

Central to the design of PKM is the concept of a "part" or "product." Design information about the part is captured as well as documentation requirements from the associated program. Documentation expressed as a "Book Form Drawing" is generated by merging this information with Boeing Drafting Standards Criteria. Exhibit 4.2 illustrates the documentation production process.

The process begins with the definition of a part whose attributes are defined, manipulated, and stored by the data management utilities. As previously stated, application software can be accessed to run design analysis, and graphics programs. The organization of the documentation is then defined by creating and editing the documentation structure. Finally, during documentation production, all components are merged with criteria from the BDS to automatically format the text and generate a documentation definition file.

Exhibit 4.2   Documentation production process.

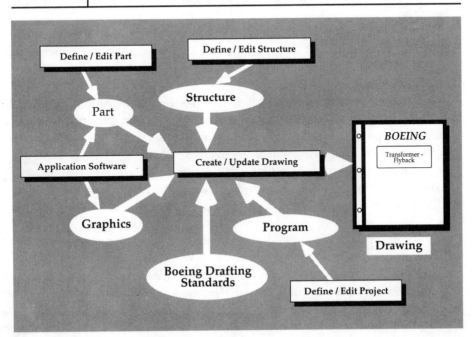

The documentation definition file information is stored in a form similar to SGML (Standard Generalized Markup Language). User print requests convert this form to Postscript for output to appropriate printers. As the documentation definition file is stored separately, changes to parts and structures will not migrate to previously created documentation unless requested by user command. Major section text is represented by a hierarchy of sections associated with that major section. Each section may contain zero or more paragraphs of text.

When producing documentation from a structure, situations arise where the specific boilerplate test supplied in a structure does not fit the requirements of the user. To handle these situations where alternative text is needed "departure sections" are used. In addition to departure sections, a second facility is available to make boilerplate text specific for one type of documentation of a part. Part attribute references can be placed in section text. When documentation is generated the attribute reference text is replaced with the value of the part attribute. This capability allows a single structure to generate unique documentation for every part.

The Structure Editor   A complete structure editor is provided within PKM. The user interface consists of a graph of the structure. Each structure object can be selected with the mouse enabling a context-sensitive menu. Functionality is provided to manipulate text sections, major sections, and departure sections as well as specific text within sections. Additionally, graphics from application software can be associated with major sections. Exhibit 4.3 shows the Structure Editor Interface.

There are numerous advantages in storing the documentation structure in a knowledge base. The ability to visually display the layout of the structure allows the user to work on the documentation from a "table of contents" viewpoint. As each section and sub-section of text are represented as objects and are members of a section object, moving a section will move all sub-sections attached to it. Therefore, any amount of text can be moved anywhere in the structure simply by moving the parent object. Copying text from one section to another is simplified to the operation of copying one object to another.

Industry standard documentation aids, such as Interleaf, PageMaker, or Context, are capable of providing many, if not all, of the functionality in the structure editor. However, a great deal of time is spent describing to the system how the page should look (changing margins, setting fonts, positioning graphics). Typically the end product is cut and pasted onto forms or a form is inserted into the printer before the documentation is printed.

The structure editor provides a controlled environment for the engineer to create special purpose documentation. It controls where text is to be placed, what approved form the text should be printed on, what fonts should be used, how paragraph numbering should be handled, along with many other formatting and

Exhibit 4.3 Structure editor interface.

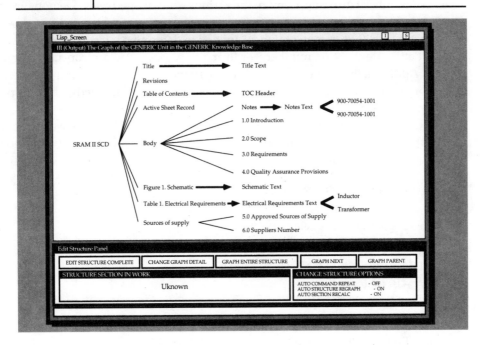

layout tasks that the user would much rather leave for someone else to do. Additionally, power users of the industry standard documentation programs became power users by virtue of continued use. As the structure editor in PKM controls the fit, form, and function of the documentation, the user is left with the task he or she is most comfortable with, that of entering the text and creating the graphics.

PKM Knowledge Bases PKM's documentation facility differs from other knowledge-based systems implementation. It uses information received from the user plus information contained in its knowledge bases to control the generation of documentation. No rules are used.

In addition to the knowledge bases required for the documentation structures, numerous others exist within PKM. These store knowledge relating to command security, user authorization, application software interface requirements, part and documentation categorization and system commands. By initiating system commands from the system control panel users may store, collect, and retrieve knowledge from PKM knowledge bases.

Beyond Object Orientation   PKM does not utilize rules. All functions are initiated by the user when a command is executed. The structure editor fully utilizes the object orientation of the structured knowledge base. Beyond the object orientation utilized by the structure editor and the user interface PKM exploits the use of inheritance and demons in various knowledge bases. Demons in the structured knowledge bases are fired whenever text in an object is altered. Any text that is modified is immediately examined to determine if it contains references to part attributes, section numbers, or formatting codes, and appropriate action is taken. Additionally, single and multiple inheritance is used in the parts knowledge base program. Form, documentation, and authorization knowledge can all provide values for part attributes.

Exhibit 4.4 lists the major components of PKM. All GUI objects were derived from the existing GUI class library. The system has 600 functions, 100 methods, 200 classes, and 500 instances.

BASIC OO FUNCTIONALITY
  – Classes/Instances.
  – Inheritance/specialization.
  – Methods/messages.

ADVANCED OO FUNCTIONALITY
  – Persistent objects.
  – Dynamic class/method generation.
  – Constraint programming.

EXTENDED PROGRAMMING ENVIRONMENT
  – Functional programming.
  – Inference/rule-based programming.

DEVELOPMENT ENVIRONMENT
  – Graphical developer interface.
  – Interpreted internal language.
  – Graphical browsers.
  – Automatic method tracing.
  – Automatic links to databases. (Via OS)
  – Internal/external class libraries. (Internal)
  – Editors.
  – Graphical tool for user interface development.
  – Tools for target operating system interface layout available.

STORAGE MANAGEMENT
  – Repository available.
  – Version control available. (created in LISP)

CODE GENERATION
  – Language code generated.
  – Compiled code generated.

Exhibit 4.4   System components.

	Hardware	Software
Interface	Apollo/HP DN4500	Mentor CAD Tools
Core Code	Apollo/HP DN4500	KEE
Database	Apollo/HP DN4500	Mentor CAD Tools
Development Environment	Apollo/HP DN4500	KEE

PROJECT LIFE CYCLE

Analysis and Design

An initial attempt to address the problem dealt with magnetics device core selection. This software was written in M.1 on IBM PCs. The system, while fulfilling the customers' initial requirements, failed to solve what some believed to be the real problem, that of device design.

A second attempt to address device design was initiated and outgrew the capabilities of M.1. The system was moved to S.1 on an 11/780 VAX. This version performed magnetics device design using active equations. It was converted to KEE in order to provide mouse-driven graphic interface. However, as with the previous attempt, this solution failed to address the problem of the entire product life cycle and its associated documentation.

Finally, the third attempt (written in KEE on a Xerox 1186) began to address product life cycle issues. This system was moved to the Apollo platform (still written in KEE) in order to utilize machines that were available to the user.

After nearly two years of prototypes and interim solutions the overall problem was redefined and as follows:

1. Existing documentation generation methods are not responsive to rigorous format and structure requirements. Each program and customer imposes constraints on the documentation and the data. The data must be consistent across the documentation. There is no facility that ensures that these re-

quirements are followed and incorporated in the documentation. No other tool, besides cut and paste, provides this functionality. Configuration control and revision control are required.

2. No defined flow/control of data existed. In the past, designs were sometimes created to a particular set of requirements and tested by another. No system provided tracking of products to determine how it performed and whether or not it should be used again. No documentation of problem processes was available or maintained. No facility to compare new requirements to past designs existed to accommodate reusability. No single database existed to hold the product knowledge attributes and allow for intelligent queries.

3. No single system was available to perform all functions required by the user. An integrated environment utilizing an intelligent front end is required. Numerous application software tools were needed for design support, analysis, and simulation. These tools ran on different platforms, required unique data formats, and had different user interfaces. The users are engineers, technicians, and documentation personnel, not computer scientists; they might not have understood how or when to execute the tools, nor be familiar with the hardware each tool ran on. No process or procedural sequence existed for running design verification programs. Tools were not being used due to lack of awareness of their existence.

Development

Peter A. Baird was the overseeing manager for development of PKM. Gregory L. Smith was the system designer and programmer. The elapsed time of the project was four years and required 8,000+ person hours.

KEE was chosen based on the following needs: workstation ability, O/S I/F facility, a GUI builder, procedural language, rules, objects methods, and because time was critical. Smith found that the documentation structure system was simple to implement using an object system.

The system consists of 600 LISP functions. The code is divided about evenly among documentation generation, structure manipulation, system and application interfaces, and the user interface.

Deployment

Deployment was relatively simple, using both interactive sessions with development personnel and training classes. The only user acceptance issue was that some users had to be taught to use a mouse.

A factor contributing to the long period of system availability and deployment is attributed to the use of KEE as a delivery platform. KEE on the Apollo provides an extremely strong development environment. However, Intellicorp did not address a delivery system on this platform. To this end, numerous LISP functions had to be generated to shield the users from KEE operations.

Maintenance

Smith describes maintenance of PKM as surprisingly minimal. The majority of knowledge in each of the knowledge bases can be modified (depending on security requirements) directly by the user. Interaction with the system is controlled by the level of the user. The system maintains three levels of users: normal end users, system administrators, and system developers.

End users have the ability to manipulate knowledge in part, structure, and documentation knowledge bases. System administrators have the added ability to manipulate forms, security, authorization, program, topology, and part type knowledge bases. System developers have control over the system command and user interface knowledge bases. They also have the only access to system function code and developer facilities (compiling, loading, and changing LISP code).

BENEFITS

According to Smith:

> It is difficult to accurately estimate savings attributable to this system. However, in the magnetics area alone (our target environment) over 200 devices are created and modified each year. Each of these devices requires over a half dozen different types of documentation. It has been estimated that using conventional word processing techniques one document or drawing can take up to 40 hours to generate. PKM has generated documentation in about three hours on the average, and in many cases has reduced that to a half hour. Additional savings attributable to the integrated user environment and improved quality, completeness, and standardization of documentation is substantial but difficult to quantify.

CONCLUSIONS

In retrospect, many of the miscommunications between developers, managers, and users stemmed from a lack of understanding as to what could be done with knowledge-based systems and what the real problem was. End users and managers did not know the strengths and capabilities of knowledge-based systems, hence could not request specific functionality (as shown by the length of time between production availability and deployment). Through incremental development methods, users and managers gained background in knowledge-based systems, and the developers gained a deeper understanding of the application.

CHAPTER 5

Application Description

WIREWRAP DESIGN SYSTEM

STATEMENT OF THE PROBLEM

1. The Wirewrap Process   Boeing Defense & Space Group is involved in developing ground support equipment and test equipment for military and commercial avionics. One of their customer requirements is the flexibility to change assemblies in the field using wirewrap technology. This wirewrap process had been in place for a number of years and needed improvement.

In the previous wirewrap process, the design schematics were captured using the standard Mentor Graphics NetEd tool. The physical layout of the wirewrap board was captured using a highly customized version of NetEd. This information was extracted into files that were then passed to another organization. This outside support organization uses an IBM mainframe to generate the body of the engineering drawing and for manufacturing a shopaid and Numeric Control data. The body of the engineering drawing along with a plot of the board layout was inserted by drafting into a wirebook drawing that specifies the configuration of the wirewrap board. The Numeric Control data was passed to yet another organization to generate the mylar punch tape that was used to drive the Gardner-Denver wirewrap machine on which the board was actually wrapped. The old process involved three organizations as shown in Exhibit 5.1.

These outside support organizations burdened the process with communications overhead and manual data preparation tasks. The process was streamlined by distributing it to the end users in circuit design groups and automating it.

2. The Engineering Change Cycle   The existing wirewrap process had an error rate of less than 1% for the initial production of a board. When changing an assembly, engineering had to redline the schematics, manually making additions and deletions to the wire list and changes to the card layout. This manual process introduced a 5% design error rate, most of which involved the creation of the add and delete lists. The paper was then sent to manufacturing where the boards were rewired manually, introducing a 5% manufacturing error rate.

Exhibit 5.1   The old design process.

Old "Over-the-Wall" Development Process Involving Three Organizations

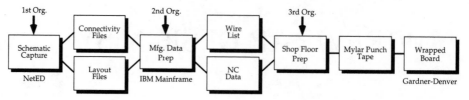

This high error rate caused the circuit designer to spend more time debugging the board. Since the configuration of the board was controlled only by the wirebook, schematics were often updated after the fact, leading to undesirable inconsistencies between the schematic and the wirebook.

SOLUTION: THE WIREWRAP DESIGN SYSTEM

The WireWrap Design System is a design automation tool used to generate the wirelist and manufacturing data needed to build or modify wirewrap designs. WWDS is composed of two major portions.

The first is an interactive wirewrap design environment based on Mentor Graphics' Boardstation product line. This environment provides an easy-to-learn user interface that is Motif compliant. Boardstation uses Mentor Graphics' Design Data Management System (DDMS), a C++ based object-oriented database. In conjunction with Mentor's Design Manager, DDMS is used to access the wirewrap design data and define versions of the design to be used for modifications. Exhibit 5.2 shows the new design process.

In the new process, a slightly modified version of Mentor Graphics' ProtoView running on the engineer's workstation is used to define the layout of the wirewrap

Exhibit 5.2   The new design process.

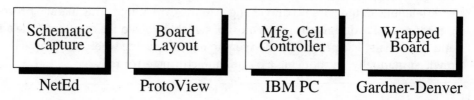

board. Custom software then replaces the IBM mainframe for engineering and manufacturing data preparation. The manufacturing data is then sent directly to a cell controller on the shop floor that drives the Gardner-Denver machine, eliminating the need for mylar tape.

The Mentor Graphics' ProtoView product is a subset of the full printed circuit board layout product, Boardstation, and is intended to be used by engineers for critical packaging and placement. Since trace routing is not required for wirewrap layout, using ProtoView significantly saves costs per new workstation. The Mentor Graphics Falcon Framework architecture greatly reduced the effort to add the wirewrap functionality to ProtoView.

The second part of the WireWrap Design System is a custom application that uses the DDMS database generated by Boardstation and creates additional design objects representing the clips and wires in the wirewrap design. The user interface for this portion is based on Mentor Graphics common user interface objects. These objects are used in the creation of engineering wirebook drawings and manufacturing reports. Report generation is achieved using a collection of approximately nine objects that represent the information in the drawing. This was done in such a manner that the user may specify any type of textual based drawing or part of a drawing that they wish. The drawing object then renders itself as a PostScript file. The DDMS drawing object specifies how the drawing is to be generated and by printing the drawing object, the PostScript file is generated.

The ability to create modification engineering reports and manufacturing data is accomplished by determining the differences between two Design Manager configurations of the wirewrap design. These differences and some manufacturing rules are used to create manufacturing data allowing the incorporation of the modifications. This has created significant savings in cost and flow time. Formerly, the information required to wirewrap boards was generated on Apollo workstations and an IBM mainframe. The new system reduces the number of computers and computer systems required, lowers the cost, and lowers the time required to wirewrap a board.

The custom portion of the WireWrap Design System is a completely object-oriented design. The design contains approximately 40 objects and has been found to be robust. Exhibit 5.3 shows the WireWrap system's domain chart.

In the new process, a slightly modified version of Mentor Graphics' ProtoView running on the engineer's workstation is used to define the layout of the wirewrap board. Custom software then replaces the IBM mainframe for engineering and manufacturing data preparation.

Exhibit 5.4 lists WDS' major components. The wirewrap-specific software was written using C + + elements of the Mentor Graphics Falcon Framework including the Common User Interface, and the Design Data Management System.

To reduce the error rate in the change process, manual, paper-based steps had to be automated. The approach taken was to track the initial configuration of the

Exhibit 5.3   Domain chart.

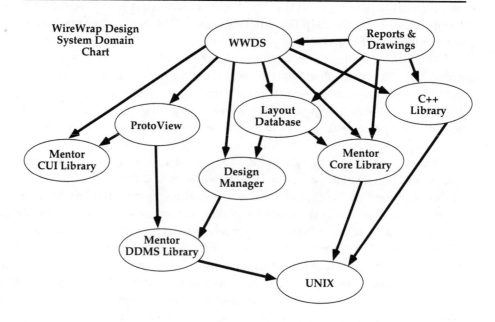

WireWrap Design
System Domain
Chart

Exhibit 5.4   System components.

	Hardware	Software
Interface	PC	Turbo Pascal
Core Code	HP 400	CFront
Database	HP 400	DDMS
Development Environment	HP 400	CFront Ample Borland C + + , Turbo Pascal

board and compare that to any new configurations. This comparison generated any change information. The configuration of the board, both the schematic and wirebook, was now controlled by the users. This new functionality was implemented in the Falcon Framework Design Manager tool.

Now, the engineer changes the design using the same tools as for the initial production of the board, rather than redlining the paper schematics or layouts. The Design Manager creates a new configuration from the modified design, then compares the new configuration with the current configuration of the board and automatically generates the add and delete list. This data is then used to generate the information that drives the Gardner-Denver machine to remove wires in an unwrap step and add the new wires.

This has automated the wirewrap change process, reduced the flow time, eliminated the wiring errors, and improved configuration management. The open architecture and configuration management services of the Falcon Framework saved the project considerable implementation effort.

WireWrap Design System employs the following OO features:

BASIC OO FUNCTIONALITY
- Classes/instances
- Inheritance/specialization
- Methods/messages
- Virtual methods/polymorphism

ADVANCED OO FUNCTIONALITY
- Persistent objects

DEVELOPMENT ENVIRONMENT
- Interpreted internal language: Mentor's Ample Language
- Internal/external class libraries

STORAGE MANAGEMENT
- Repository available
- Version control available

PROJECT LIFE CYCLE

Analysis Design and Development

The decision to change the wirewrap process began with the circuit designers themselves. Via an employee suggestion system, the first step was to form a process improvement team. This mixed-discipline team, made up of designers, assemblers, and software support, defined the requirements. They assessed the current process, planned improvements, then implemented the automation of the new process. They recognized the need for revolutionary, not evolutionary, changes in their tools. The second step was to sell the need for change to management. This was done over a six-month evaluation period. Once educated about the issues, management was very supportive.

The commercial wirewrap software available was studied and none was found that met the requirements. Contracting with a vendor to develop the software was investigated but it was determined that coordinating the outside development would be as big a task as developing the software in-house.

Both engineering and manufacturing had numerous and very specific requirements. For example, from the engineering side, the process had to meet drafting standards, provide configuration control, allow flexibility, and ensure that quality is built in and not added on. From the manufacturing side came requirements to follow strict formats for the NC data and how the data gets to the shop floor, and to follow standards for component library information so that printed circuit board and wirewrap layout could use the same parts libraries.

In some cases the initial requirements derived by the process improvement team were too specific. Each member of this team, chosen because of intimate familiarity with the process, suggested detailed requirements for functionality as well as for implementation—both the "what" and the "how." These implementation details tended not to take advantage of the new capabilities in the Falcon Framework. To revise the requirements document, implementation requirements had to be filtered out so that only functionality requirements were addressed.

Everything about the design environment was new, except the wirewrap technology. The new process uses all new vendor software and C++. Training in this new environment was critical to the success of a quality product. The four members of the team charged with implementing the software for the new process took C++ and OpenDoor toolkit courses from Mentor Graphics and a series of three one-week courses on object-oriented design and analysis techniques from Project Technology, Inc. The entire team took an in-house process management class on Total Quality Improvement, early in the process. This training significantly shortened the learning curve, improved the quality of the final software, and allowed for some team building.

State models were simulated using software created internally by Greg Smith. Fifteen person months have been required so far for A&D and development.

Deployment

The system is in limited production. It has produced a number of boards, but, according to Keenan, it is still in advanced beta test.

BENEFITS

Faster: In the previous process to rework a board, 40% of the time was spent redlining the wire list, another 20% was spent in the shop manually reworking the assembly, and another 40% of the time was spent troubleshooting and reworking the board. The team was able to reduce all these steps to 20% of the original amount of time.

Cheaper: The cost to manually generate a wirebook drawing was significantly more than the automated process. Also, the cost of a typical change was significantly reduced. The ability to rapidly turn around engineering changes saves additional costs when those changes are on the customer's critical path. This cost can be significant if it is holding up a project. The open architecture of the Mentor Graphics tools and the Falcon Framework significantly reduced the implementation cost of the wirewrap system, thus making in-house development a viable option.

Better: The automation of the engineering change cycle reduced the combined engineering and manufacturing error rate of 10% to less than 1%. This not only means that the wirewrap board gets built as designed but also dramatically reduces unnecessary handling of the board and reduces the chance that the board will be damaged. The new wirewrap process also ensures the consistency of the design database because schematics are updated before changes to the board are made, instead of after the fact. The quality of the wirewrap application software itself benefited through the use of object-oriented design, as demonstrated by the ability to respond quickly to requirement changes and to make those changes right the first time.

CONCLUSIONS

Asked what advice he'd give others contemplating similar efforts, Keenan was cautionary:

> OO is a two-edged sword. You have to invest enough time up front. Most of the people I've talked to say that C++ makes a good programmer better and a bad programmer worse. OO is not foolproof.

CHAPTER 6

Application Description

CZ PROTOCOL PRINT

STATEMENT OF THE PROBLEM

Wacker Siltronic manufactures silicon wafers that are sold to integrated circuit manufacturers. These wafers are cut from meter-long crystals grown in computer controlled furnaces containing molten silicon. Growing these crystals is tricky because of the many variations in the ways crystals are grown. Wacker manages and continually improves upon many recipes (called processes) for controlling these furnaces.

Likewise, Wacker's customers purchase wafers with different kinds of properties and characteristics, based on the kind of integrated circuit to be manufactured. They purchase from Wacker wafers grown to a particular "product line." The relationship between product line and process is complex. One product line might be satisfied by any number of processes. The process selected depends on many factors such as the type of dopant material available, time to grow, and the scheduling of other orders with compatible product line characteristics.

To tell the people loading the furnace which combination of ingredients and which furnace settings to use, a CZ Protocol Sheet was hand-written by a senior person known as a scheduler. Using this protocol sheet, the computer controlling the furnace was programmed by hand for each crystal. Hand entry was error prone, about one crystal a month was misprogrammed. The material wasted ranged from $3,000 to $6,000. Added to this was the lost capacity (about 24 hours) of the major bottleneck section in the manufacturing line, the cost of the personnel running the furnace, the cost of discovering the mistake, the cost of rescheduling the crystal, and disruption of the planned shipping goals of departments further down the line.

Wacker's goal was to automate the jobs of scheduling and programming the furnace. It also needed to automate the jobs of creating and refining new processes and product lines. The program needed to be defect-free in two ways: it could not misprogram the furnace, and it could not let a scheduler accidentally specify growing characteristics that were out of the known ranges for successful crystals. The program was to be used daily, in the key area of the manufacturing line, so its maintenance had to be close to nil.

The program had to be easy to learn because the end-users had no special computer skills. It was a human interface intensive problem in that the variation in the process and the product lines was vast. It was a database intensive problem in that the relationships between the product lines and the processes were not regular, and both product lines and processes had to be easily modified.

It was also seen as a multiple object constraints problem in the need to assure that there were no conflicts between multiple product lines for a selected process.

SOLUTION: CZ PROTOCOL PRINT

Given these requirements, Wacker decided to use a methodical object-oriented approach. Their analysis included Information Modeling (Shlaer), entity-state modeling, event-partitioned data flow modeling, (McMinaman), and three-dimensional human interface perspective modeling (3D-HIP), by Kerth. Their design methodology was multiple-views object-oriented design (MOOD).

Objects were used extensively. The human interface was built of objects and had objects within objects. A generic view object was created once and reused widely. Likewise, warning messages and labeled fill-outs, and the human interface part were written once and used often. The human interface intensive aspects of the program were very low cost, due to this reuse.

Each process and product line became an object that needed to be persistent. They were stored in collections that hid the database implementation that provided persistence. The barcode generator was an object that knew how to print the three-by-nine industry standard barcode.

The operation of CZ Protocol Print can be seen in the following screen shots:

Exhibit 6.1. CZ Protocol.
This is the main output of the program.

Exhibit 6.2. Process Code Manager.
This is the main screen. Selecting A will cause the ASSOCIATE PROCESS TO . . . screen to display. Selecting C will cause the PROCESS NUMBER TO BE . . . to display.

Exhibit 6.3. Associate Process To Prod . . .
The scheduler indicates the product line to be selected. Given this information, the program determines the heat treatment and calculates the preferred process

Exhibit 6.1 CZ protocol.

	Product Line	Furnace	Ingot Number
	UH12		611730

CZ PROTOCOL

BORON   1 – 1 – 1
P1128T129   09130113
10. 308. 23   105 722
Funnel: 300 x 280 x 228   Orifice: 280 x 200
Hotzone Setup: T 28

Date/Time: 19 May 1992 14: 39: 0

Purge Tube Dim.   110 x 160 x 342
Diameter: 129.0
Cruc. Lift: 0 .204

Max Body Length: 82.0
Cool Time: 180
Heat Treat: INGOT

Seed Lift   1.7 e0, 1.7 e30, 1.6 e55, 1.4 e75, 1.4 e200
Seed RPM   15. 0 e0, 15. 0 e150
max CR RPM   5.0 e0, 5.0 e160
min CR RPR
Argon   675 e0, 675 e200
Pressure   18. 0 e0, 18.0 e10, 11.0 e40, 8.0 e60, 8.0 e200

FURNACE/HOTZONE

	Vendor/Serial	Runs	Outbake/New
Heater			
Susc.			
Base			
Heat Shield			
Moly Cone			

New Felt   Top: Bottom:
      Heatshield:
Crucible Position   Start: End:
Crucible Position   Start: End:
Power Neck:
Rollover MM:
Meltback Dia MM:
Meltback Length MM:
Termination Code:
Hot Leak MBAR:
Defect Free CM:
PTs In:
PTs Out:
Seed 3   In: Out:
rho Top: 15. 00   Bottom: 2. 00

PROCESS DEVIATIONS

PACKING

Polyrod	Ohm-CM		G
Poly 6	Ohm-CM		G
Poly 5	Ohm-CM		G
Poly 4	Ohm-CM		G
Poly 3	Ohm-CM		G
Dopart 0.00249	Ohm-CM	0. 82	G

Target 14.0000   Total Weight   28000.00   G
Dopant Ingot: Dopant Check:

OD xH MM	Crucible Vendor	Lot Number
330 x 240		
Pack Date:	By:	

GROWING

	Grow Start	Grow End	
Date			
Time			
OPERATION	Start Time	Period	Operator #
Setup/Eval			
Meltdown			
Dip-In			
Body			
Contraction			
Recharge			
Dip-In			
Body			
Endcone			
Cool			
Removal			
Total Time			
Anneal			Unit #

Exhibit 6.2 Process code manager.

PROCESS CODE MANAGER
     VERSION 2.2.4 OF CZDEFNPR.EXE   -5/14/92

Commands

^A   :   Associate Process to
         a Product Line

^C   :   Clone or Edit a Process

^N   :   New Process

^Q   :   Quit

Exhibit 6.3   Associate product to process.

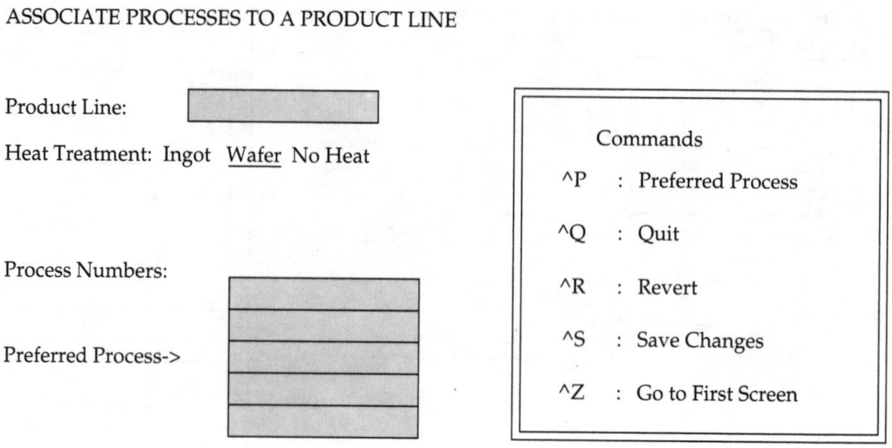

ASSOCIATE PROCESSES TO A PRODUCT LINE

Product Line: [   ]

Heat Treatment: Ingot <u>Wafer</u> No Heat

```
                                    ┌─────────────────────────────────────┐
                                    │ ┌─────────────────────────────────┐ │
                                    │ │         Commands                │ │
Process Numbers:                    │ │                                 │ │
           ┌───────────────┐        │ │  ^P   :  Preferred Process      │ │
           │               │        │ │                                 │ │
           ├───────────────┤        │ │  ^Q   :  Quit                   │ │
Preferred Process->        │        │ │                                 │ │
           ├───────────────┤        │ │  ^R   :  Revert                 │ │
           │               │        │ │                                 │ │
           ├───────────────┤        │ │  ^S   :  Save Changes           │ │
           │               │        │ │                                 │ │
           └───────────────┘        │ │  ^Z   :  Go to First Screen     │ │
                                    │ └─────────────────────────────────┘ │
                                    └─────────────────────────────────────┘
```

and provides any alternative processes that would also be applicable. The scheduler then selects the process best suited to current circumstances.

Exhibit 6.4. Process Number To Be . . .

This is the "work horse" screen used by the process engineers to create new processes or refine existing ones.

Exhibit 6.5 lists the main components of CZ Protocol Print. CZ Protocol Print employs the following OO features:

BASIC OO FUNCTIONALITY
– Classes/instances.
– Inheritance/specialization.
– Methods/messages.
– Virtual methods/polymorphism.

ADVANCED OO FUNCTIONALITY
– Persistent objects.

CODE GENERATION
– Compiled code generated.

Exhibit 6.4   Process number to be.

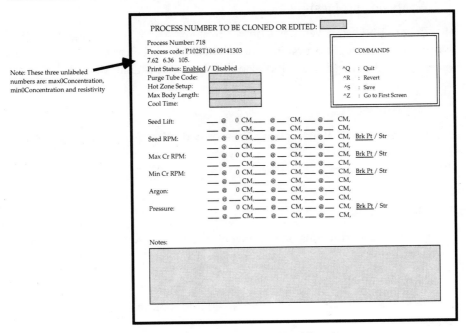

PROCESS NUMBER TO BE CLONED OR EDITED:

Process Number: 718
Process code: P1028T106 09141303
7.62 6.36 105.
Print Status: <u>Enabled</u> / Disabled
Purge Tube Code:
Hot Zone Setup:
Max Body Length:
Cool Time:

COMMANDS

^Q : Quit
^R : Revert
^S : Save
^Z : Go to First Screen

Note: These three unlabeled numbers are: max0Concentration, min0Concentration and resistivity

Seed Lift: __ @ 0 CM,__ @ __ CM, __ @ __ CM,
                __ @ __ CM,__ @ __ CM, __ @ __ CM,
Seed RPM: __ @ 0 CM,__ @ __ CM, __ @ __ CM, <u>Brk Pt</u> / Str
                __ @ __ CM,__ @ __ CM, __ @ __ CM,
Max Cr RPM: __ @ 0 CM,__ @ __ CM, __ @ __ CM, <u>Brk Pt</u> / Str
                __ @ __ CM,__ @ __ CM, __ @ __ CM,
Min Cr RPM: __ @ 0 CM,__ @ __ CM, __ @ __ CM, <u>Brk Pt</u> / Str
                __ @ __ CM,__ @ __ CM, __ @ __ CM,
Argon: __ @ 0 CM,__ @ __ CM, __ @ __ CM,
                __ @ __ CM,__ @ __ CM, __ @ __ CM,
Pressure: __ @ 0 CM,__ @ __ CM, __ @ __ CM, <u>Brk Pt</u> / Str
                __ @ __ CM,__ @ __ CM, __ @ __ CM,

Notes:

Note: the cursor is not in one of the fields that can be either a break point field or a string field (Brk Pt / Str). The Commands box changes when the cursor moves into one of those fields. See Views 4.1 and 4.1.1.

Exhibit 6.5   System components.

	Hardware	*Software*
Interface	IBM PC comp	Turbo Pascal V5.5
Core Code	IBM PC comp	Turbo Pascal V5.5
Database	IBM PC comp	Turbo Pascal V5.5 & Paradox Engine
Development Environment	IBM PC comp 386	Turbo Pascal V5.5

PROJECT LIFE CYCLE

Analysis and Design

Robert Rhodes, a Wacker Control Systems Engineer, managed the project. Norman Kerth, of Elite Systems, developed the specification and design methodology used in the project, and also did the systems analysis and design.

Development

The program contains 20,000 lines of code. Robert Rhodes wrote approximately 25% of the code, the rest was written by John Burley of Victory Software. The cost of development was approximately $40,000.

Deployment

CZ Protocol Print runs on one machine, and is used by five employees.

Maintenance

The program has required less than 40 hours of maintenance in the past two years.

BENEFITS

CZ Protocol Print has made the scheduler's job much easier. It takes less than a week for a new scheduler to learn how to use the program. It calls their attention to any theoretically unreasonable protocol definitions by deploying a complex algorithm. Schedulers use the program every day, but for only about 5% of their time. Before the program existed the same tasks took them nearly full time, to the neglect of other responsibilities. Schedulers are now free to deal with the more pressing problem of process improvement.

The application has improved the manufacturing process, saving the company $33,000 to $72,000 per year in materials alone, achieving a positive return on investment in a few months. Overall, the average direct benefits of this system for over 28 months have been: materiel savings of $140,000, and labor savings of $48,000.

The benefits of object-oriented technology are enormous, according to Rhodes and Kerth:

> The part of the benefit that is attributable to OO is difficult to estimate. We feel that the primary benefit has nothing to do with the cost savings generated by the application. Any application can be written without OO. The benefit comes

from the ease of development, the quality of the resulting system, and the ease of later modifications. Since a class library was not used in this application, we do not feel that the application was significantly easier to develop, we do feel that the quality of the result, as reflected by the very low number of bugs, and the low maintenance costs was greater. We estimate that the database modifications would have taken twice as long to implement, thus a cost of approximately $4,200 was avoided. Lower maintenance costs will be incurred throughout the life of this application, and that is due to OO.

We also found that methodically analyzing the problem and designing an object-oriented solution with well defined boundaries created a defect-free system. Out of the 20,000 lines of code, acceptance testing found only four defects. The program has been used every day for the past two years in a plant that runs 24 hours a day, seven days a week, and no defects have been found.

Within our department, this experience has raised our expectations of what we thought was reasonable software engineering productivity. We have created new corporate software development standards that call for more precise analysis and design activities similar to the ones used on this project.

CONCLUSIONS

Rhodes sees the acceptance of OO at Wacker as a gradual process:

> To be honest, a great deal of training must occur before we see our experiences shared widely across the company. Nevertheless, we have a vision, we have a successful pilot project, we have impressive statistics, and we have the attention of a few aggressive managers. If we can get the attention of software engineers across the company and they too can deploy object-oriented technology successfully, the cost savings to the company will be incredible!

Acknowledgment   As Wacker Siltronic's first OO project they needed to leverage outside expertise. Norm Kerth is a consultant who specializes in successful transitions to OO technologies. Mr. Kerth was a major factor both in the success of this project and in the speed with which Wacker Siltronic staff were able to master this new technology.

Domain:
Software Development

A s a rule, the industry that is quickest to adopt new software technologies is the software development industry. Software companies create software for a living. For the more-established software vendors, constant maintenance and enhancement are the keys. For newer, smaller software vendors, innovative programs that are visually impressive and significantly more efficient are the key to breaking into the highly competitive marketplace.

Just behind the software vendors themselves are the advanced technology groups located inside large companies. These groups are charged with exploring new technologies and developing new tools that their corporate software developers can use to maintain their corporate software resources.

When most people think of object technology, they think of graphical user interfaces on PCs. Software developers, vendors and corporate developers alike, have been quick to exploit the GUI capabilities of object technology to create better interfaces for their users. At the same time, however, people who develop software for a living are aware of object technologies' other uses—to facilitate better code maintenance and reuse, to facilitate better-designed client-server applications, and to support better analysis and design efforts. These other advantages of object technology are just as relevant to mainframe and workstation developers as they are to PC developers. We have chosen five applications to illustrate some of the uses of object technology within the software development community.

Landschaftsverband Rheinland (LVR) is a German organization that maintains and develops many large software applications on IBM mainframes. To keep track of all of the software modules that the company uses in its many different projects, LVR created an OO system, Configuration Management System (CMS). The problem was analyzed and designed using OO techniques. The actual software was created using C/370 and DB2. This application illustrates the value of OO A&D, independent of the language used to implement the application. It also illustrates the successful use of OO in a mainframe environment.

In a similar application in the United States, IBM used object technology to create a system to keep track of software components so developers can quickly find components when they are needed. IBM has used OO A&D and an OO language, Smalltalk, to create a workstation-based Reuse Support System for their software developers.

Boeing Defense & Space Group is part of a company that has long been a leader in the application of new software technologies to aerospace and computer problems, both for themselves and for their clients. In the mid-1980s, for example, Boeing was one of the first companies to explore and benefit from the use of AI and expert system techniques. Thus, when faced with a CAD application that called for object technology, one Boeing group immediately realized that the OO techniques they had already been using in expert systems development could assist them in the OO development area. Boeing used an object-based expert system building tool to create an interactive development environment in which new applications could be incrementally developed and tested. Now, in the 1990s, several OO vendors are enhancing their OO 4GL and CASE tools to include interpreted analysis and design environments. Boeing, however, is already enjoying the advantages of combining expert system tools and OO to create a powerful new approach to rapid application development.

In still another example of the use of OO, Micro Focus Inc., a software vendor, has used object technology to enhance their Micro Focus Workbench product. They have used Smalltalk V to create a PC-based tool that fine-tunes existing COBOL applications to assure that they make efficient use of mainframe resources.

NeXT Computers, like any company, has a software group that develops software to help their internal people keep track of data. The head of IS at NeXT used NeXT's OO NeXTSTEP product to create an electronic form to speed up purchase recquisitions. It was so popular that it led to several more requests. Rather than devote his life to creating electronic forms, the manager created a meta-tool, Formkit, that made it easy for departmental people to create their own electronic forms. This product certainly relies on a good GUI to facilitate its use by the departmental developers and the subsequent users. It also illustrates the power of object techniques to make it easy to reuse code.

As the examples in this chapter illustrate, the analysis and design power, and the simulation and pattern-matching advantages of object technology, make it a natural choice for complex applications that need to keep track of many different components. The examples also suggest how object techniques can create better code on mainframes and workstations as well as on PCs. Object technology is not just pretty: it is powerful, as these serious software development applications illustrate.

CHAPTER 7

Application Description

OBJECT-ORIENTED ANALYSIS SIMULATOR

Boeing Defense & Space Group in Seattle has developed a PC-based OO CASE tool using IntelliCorp's Kappa-PC, an expert-system-building tool. The tool was developed by Boeing in conjunction with another application described in this book, the WireWrap Design System.

STATEMENT OF THE PROBLEM

When Boeing decided to use an object-oriented programming methodology on a new CAD project, WireWrap Design System (WWD), OOP methodology was new to the organization. As the system design proceeded, in-depth knowledge of the system was needed. Much of the OO design documents were difficult to readily understand and their content was sometimes inconsistent. It was also difficult to visualize the execution of the system and how the objects would interact.

For the WWD system the Shlaer-Mellor methodology from Project Technologies Inc. was used. The methodology is a recursive application of object-oriented analysis and design. In developing OO applications tools are required to maintain consistency between objects, data, and their relationships. If a strong representation of the OO analysis knowledge is available in the tool, simulation of the analysis is possible. An OOA simulation can then identify errors in the design concerning timing and logic long before effort is expended on coding.

SOLUTION: OBJECT-ORIENTED ANALYSIS SIMULATOR

OOA Simulator is a knowledge-based CASE tool allowing the software developer to describe an object-oriented analysis using data extracted from traditional OO documentation (information models, state diagrams, and event lists). Once the analysis has been described, the knowledge-based system can simulate the analysis by creating instances of objects, passing events between objects, and transitioning objects from state to state based on various events. The system was built with Kappa-PC, a product of IntelliCorp, Inc.

The system provides two user interfaces: a summary session and state model sessions. State model sessions are identical to the state models in the analysis. One state model session exists for each state model in the domain. As objects transition from state to state, the boxes (representing states) on the interface change color. Red signifies the object's current state, green signifies previously transitioned states, and white indicates states not transitioned to. These sessions are for display only and provide no user functionality other than the visual effect of seeing an object transition from state to state. Exhibit 7.1 shows a screen from a state model session, for an object called Clip Pin.

The summary user interface displays all the objects, the current state of the objects, the current event being processed, a system message window, and run

Exhibit 7.1   Clip pin state model session.

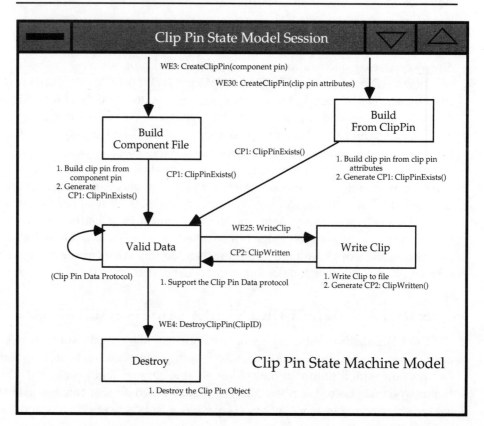

and reset actuators. When an object is selected it displays a list of either the states that object has transitioned through, or the events that the object has sent and received.

A simulation session is initiated when a user selects an event (from an event menu) and sends it to an object. Once initiated the system continues by transitioning objects and performing actions corresponding to the new state. The system halts when there are no outstanding events to be sent. At that time, the user can query the objects, or select another event to send. Exhibit 7.2 shows the screen for the summary session of the WireWrap Design System.

Knowledge Representation   Analysis objects are classified in the knowledge base as either internal (objects created and/or used in the analysis) or external (objects outside the scope of the analysis, such as data, the user, other systems). Each analysis class is represented by a class in the knowledge base. All of the instances of the analysis classes become instances of the knowledge-base class as

Exhibit 7.2   Summary session.

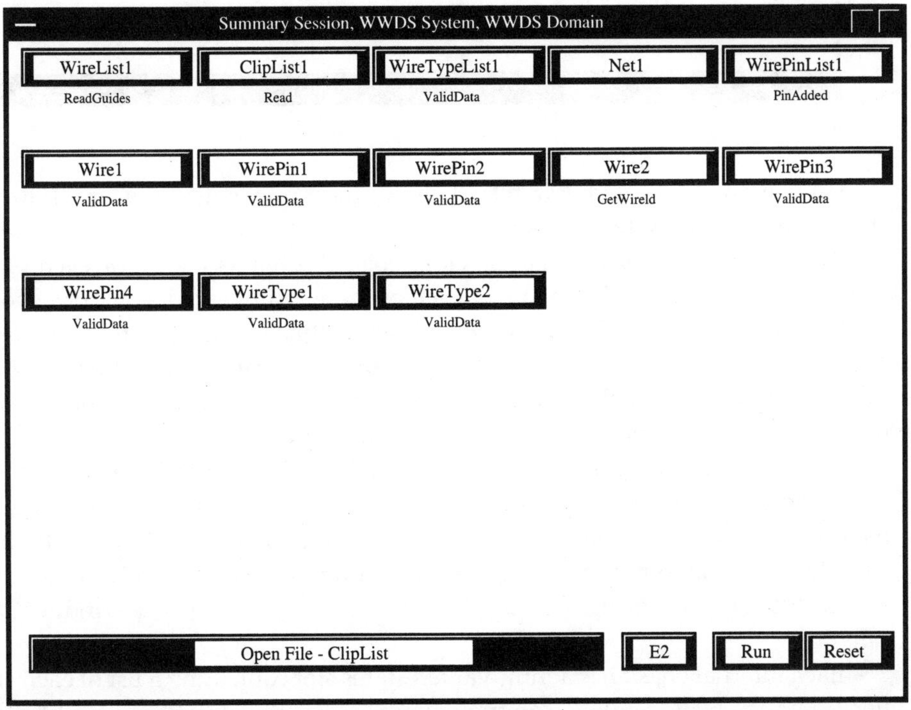

Exhibit 7.3   Knowledge base graph.

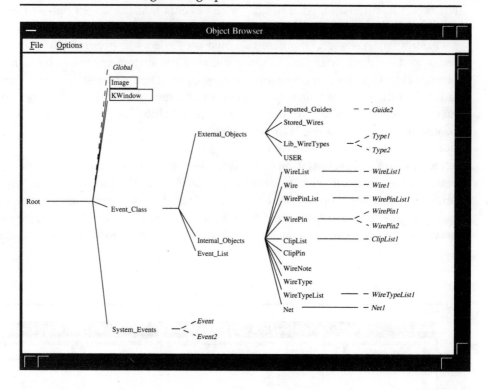

the simulation is executed. Exhibit 7.3 shows the Knowledge Base Graph for the WireWrap Design System domain.

The parent class of all analysis class objects contains a slot for each of the possible system events. The name of each of these multivalued slots corresponds to the name of an event. By placing the events at this high level in the knowledge structure they are defined in only one place and inheritance copies them down to internal objects, external objects, and the event list. For internal and external objects, the value of the event slots are instances of events that have been sent to that object. For the event list, the values of the slots describe the events. An event is described by the event type, the event source (an object class), the event destination (an object class), and the event data attributes. A facility has recently been completed that automatically imports and exports the simulator event list from and to the OOA event list residing on an Excel spreadsheet via Window DDE calls.

Each internal object has a multivalued states slot containing a list of each state (including the NULL state) it can transition to. Also, the object has a multivalued slot for each of the states. The values of these slots are legal events that allow the object to transition. This information is used to detect and alert the user should an illegal event be sent to an object in the wrong state. For historical purposes, each slot maintains a list of events that were sent to the object and states the object transitioned to as a result of the event. A status slot maintains the name of the object's current state.

A system event class is the parent of all outstanding events. When an event is sent from one object to another, a system event instance is created. This instance contains all information about the specific event: name, source instance, destination instance, attribute data, etc. The name of the instance is added to the object's corresponding slot for that particular event name. As the object event slots are lists, many identical events (most likely from different sources) can be sent to the same object. The events are queued on the list in first-in first-out order.

An interesting difference between OOA Simulator and other knowledge-based systems is that the rules are completely replaced with every analysis. The rules are used to mimic an object in a specific state. The antecedent part (the "if" part) of the rule contains an OR-ing of all possible events and the associated objects and states that will transition the object into another state. The consequent part (the "then" part) of the rule contains actions that take place once the object transitions to the new state.

A set of simulation functions were created to support the actions of objects. These functions include opening/closing/writing files, system messaging, deleting/creating objects, and so forth. These functions are executed as objects transition into new states.

State Transitioning   Transitioning objects from state to state simulates the analysis. The following list details the steps required to cycle through a state-change as shown in Exhibit 7.4:

1. An event is sent to an object (initiated by the user or the action in a state).
2. The function CREATE.EVENT creates an instance of the event called EVENT1. EVENT1 attributes include source instance, event name, and destination instance.
3. The function VALIDATE.EVENT checks the validity of the event.
4. If the event is invalid a warning is displayed to the user. If the event is valid, the function GET.ARGUMENTS is called and any required data arguments are requested from the user.
5. The SEND.EVENT function adds the event instance name to the destination object's event list.

Exhibit 7.4   System function and rules flows.

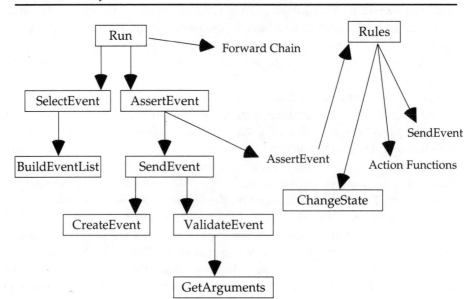

6. The event is asserted (forward chaining has previously been initiated).

7. All appropriate rules are placed on the agenda and examined. The rules check object event lists and identify any non-zero length entries.

8. If a rule antecedent is satisfied, the rule is fired. The rule calls the CHANGE.STATE function to update the state slots of the object. The rule executes the actions of the state.

9. If an action of the state is to send an event, then the system cycle repeats with this new event. If no more events are outstanding, the system halts.

The major components of OOA Simulator are shown in Exhibit 7.5. OOA Simulator has 40 functions, 10 methods, 20 classes. The number of instances and rules depends on the size of the system being simulated.

OOA Simulator has the following features:

BASIC OO FUNCTIONALITY
  – Classes/instances.
  – Inheritance/specialization.
  – Methods/messages.

ADVANCED OO FUNCTIONALITY
  – Persistent objects.
  – Constraint programming.

Exhibit 7.5   The major components of an OOA simulator.

	Hardware	Software
Interface	IBM PC comp 386	Windows DDE
Core Code	IBM PC comp 386	KAPPA-PC
Database	IBM PC comp 386	EXCEL
Development Environment	IBM PC comp 386	KAPPA-PC

EXTENDED PROGRAMMING ENVIRONMENT
  – Functional programming.
  – Inference/rule-based programming.

DEVELOPMENT ENVIRONMENT
  – Graphical developer interface.
  – Interpreted internal language.
  – Graphical browsers.
  – Automatic method tracing.
  – Automatic links to databases.
  – Internal/external class libraries.
  – Editors.
  – Graphical tool for user interface development.
  – Tools for target operating system interface layout available.

STORAGE MANAGEMENT
  – Repository available.

CODE GENERATION
  – Language code generated. (KAL can be generated.)
  – Compiled code generated.

PROJECT LIFE CYCLE

Analysis and Design

OOA Simulator was straightforward to develop due to the symmetry between event and state models of OOP and rules and objects in the knowledge-based systems world, and because of the well-defined requirements of the OOP paradigm.

Simulation is possible (once specific rules and events are defined) by simply forward chaining through the rules. The system displays timing errors, missing events, erroneous states, and non-reachable states. This capability to simulate the analysis before actual code is generated can save countless hours by illuminating possible problems long before they've reached the code.

Requirements for the development environment for this tool included: PC-based Windows operation, an object system, a forward chaining rule system, a procedural language, a user interface building facility, and DDE and DLL capability. Four expert systems shells were examined: Level5 Object, Nexpert, ADS, and Kappa-PC. While all of tools ran on a PC, Nexpert did not provide a procedural language, ADS did not run in a Windows environment, and didn't have a procedural language, and Level5 Object didn't have an object system or a procedural language. Kappa-PC provided all the required facilities.

To develop this type of system without the availability of an object system, a rule system, the forward chaining capability, and the user interface development environment would have added over a year to the development time. The added time would have made the development cycle unacceptable. Other ways would have been investigated.

Development

Costs to develop the system were minimal. All development work was performed on a 386 PC with only word processors and the Kappa-PC development environment. Functions to run the analysis simulation and create the user interface required less than three months to develop due to the symmetry between states and events in the OOA. and rules and chaining in the KB tool. Most of the development time was spent identifying rules for specific application simulations. For the WWDS domain, over 50 rules were required. For the entire WWDS system, over 250 rules were required. Development took six months and required approximately 800 hours.

Deployment

Deployment of the OOA Simulator has been limited. Only a handful of OO activities are in a stage that would benefit from the use of this tool. As new OOP projects are started and the knowledge of this tool's existence and capabilities are better advertised within the company, the OOA Simulator should see much higher utilization.

Maintenance

Maintenance is reportedly minimal.

BENEFITS

The major benefit of OOA Simulator is to identify errors in the analysis before they propagate to the code. Although numerous discrepancies were found and repaired during the analysis of the WWDS, it is not possible to quantify the savings in terms of dollars or person hours. The current version of the system uses existing OOA documentation. Rules must be extracted from this documentation. To continuously use the simulator both sets of documentation must be updated, requiring additional effort, but the effort results in the detection of errors that could have gone undetected. With the addition of Phase II, the automatic importing and exporting of the OOA documentation such duplicate effort will be eliminated. Without the overhead of maintaining two documentation sets, return-on-investment will be even greater.

CONCLUSIONS

Phase I of this application was completed in June 1991. Phase II, currently in development, will provide a simplified method of importing the analysis thus automating the rule generation process, and outputing traditional OOA documentation. Phase III will provide mapping rules between the simulator pseudo code and the implementation language. With the addition of these mapping rules, the system will attempt to generate end user code, a first step in automating the software development process.

CHAPTER 8

Application Description

REUSE SUPPORT SYSTEM

STATEMENT OF THE PROBLEM

Reusing software components requires that programmers be able to find the components quickly using terminology that is meaningful to them. Given a lab with millions of lines of code in multiple languages, products, library systems, and platforms, a developer had a nearly impossible task to find a component that was applicable to the problem at hand. It was easier to re-create the component than to locate it.

SOLUTION: THE REUSE SUPPORT SYSTEM

The Reuse Support System (RSS) is a tool to help find software components to reuse. RSS lets the user search for software by entering keyword expressions. An expression consists of keywords, categories, boolean operators, and parentheses.

- The boolean operators supported in the first release are "and," "or," "andNot," and "xor." Boolean operators are not case sensitive.

- Keywords are any alphanumeric (but not entirely numeric) string of at least two characters. Keywords must match whole words in the source (e.g. the source string "the sorting routine" contains the keyword "sorting" but not the keyword "sort"). In the second release, word roots will be handled (e.g. you could enter "sorting" and would hit on "sort," "sorts," "sorting," and "sorter," if you chose the root word option).

- Categories are collections of related keywords. Categories can also contain other categories in a hierarchical relationship.

When entering a search expression, keywords are entered beginning with a lowercase letter (or digit) and categories are entered beginning with an uppercase letter.

RSS uses pre-built indexes, called keyword dictionaries, to locate files where the specified keywords occur. Information about any files that meet the search criteria is returned to the user. The user can get, browse, or edit the referenced files. In a future release, users will also be able to supply components to a reuse library. The user must have prebuilt keyword dictionaries to perform searches against. This is necessary for requests to be answered in a reasonable amount of time, since the search could be across large volumes of data, such as all the C code in a development library for multiple products.

The RSS is primarily a workstation tool, but also has a mainframe portion, which collects information about files located there. In the first release, RSS works with the Corporate Reuse Environment mainframe library, IDSS mainframe library, VM flat files, OS/2 HPFS files, and workstation FAT files. The second release will add SCLM mainframe library, PVCS workstation library, MVS PDS, and MVS flat file. The mainframe collection process is an administrator task, run entirely on the mainframe. The PWS collection process can be done by any RSS user. It is recommended that a PWS administrator perform this time consuming background task for his or her group for shared files. Individuals are certainly free to collect information about their own personal files as well.

Exhibit 8.1 shows on overview of the RSS system architecture. The administrator task (*Admin*) is a batch process that builds the keyword dictionaries. Since RSS is geared to work against large volumes of data and still achieve fast response to expression searches, it is necessary to prebuild indexing information. The average keyword dictionary is less than 10% of the volume to the original data. The workstation code is written in Smalltalk/V PM, with some TCP/IP file transfer code written in C (and wrapped in a file transfer facility framework in Smalltalk). The *Remote Admin* code is written in REXX on the mainframe, since Smalltalk is not supported there.

The language sensitive editor, (LSE) allows users to enter keyword expressions for searches. The LSE gives immediate feedback, as keystrokes are entered, as to the status of the expression. This feedback is in the form of colors to indicate token types and invalid states.

The *Search* portion of the RSS uses an expression entered by the user to search the user's current active set of keyword dictionaries, which are accessed locally or over the network. Any resulting components that match the expression are listed for the user. The user can then retrieve or browse components. The RSS uses TCP/IP to copy the component to the user's disk and brings up his or her favorite editor, if requested.

In Exhibit 8.3, the Site that is referred to by the address information can be local or remote. Remote sites can be accessed via TCP/IP. In addition, keyword dictionaries that are distributed at remote sites can be used for searches.

Exhibit 8.1   RSS architecture overview.

Reuse Support System (RSS) Architecture
Overview

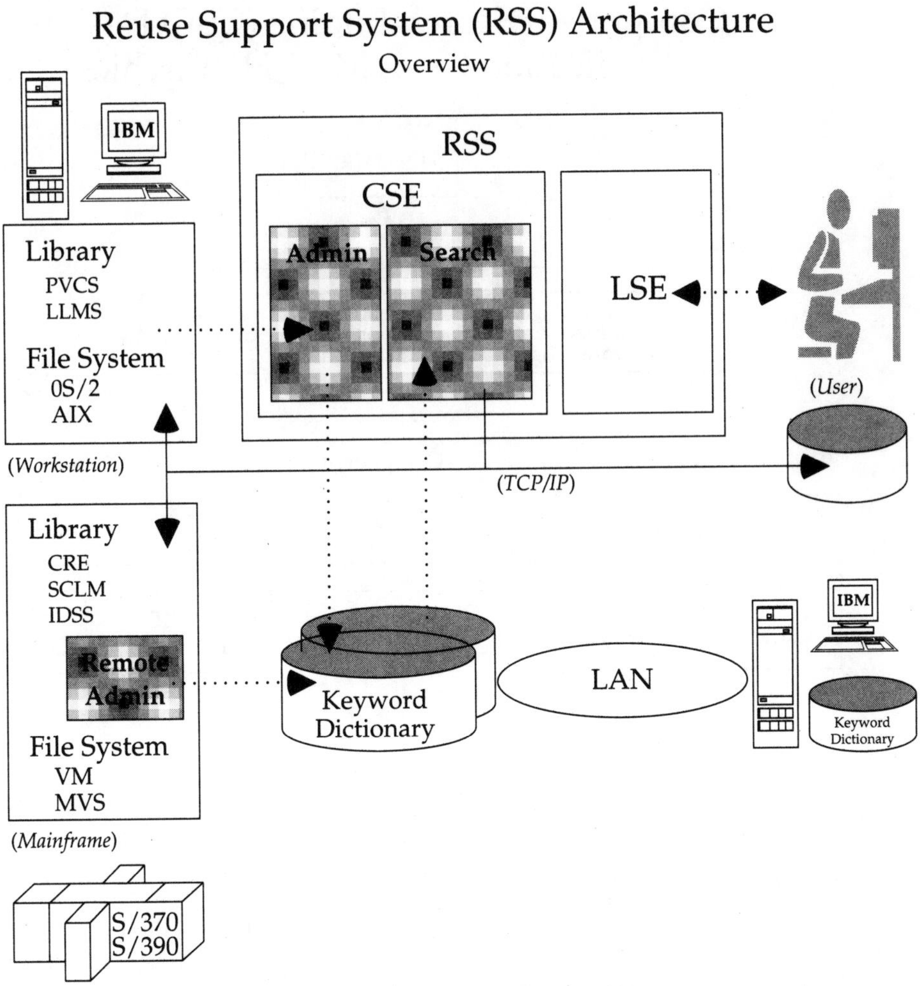

Exhibits 8.2, 8.3 and 8.4 show the object hierarchies with RSS.

RSS was built to facilitate reuse, but was also designed to be reusable itself. There are a number of components within RSS that are reusable. The largest ones are the Component Search Engine (CSE) and Language Sensitive Editor (LSE) which make up the bulk of the system, as shown in Exhibit 8.5.

An effort has begun to reuse the configuration of the original system as part of a Smalltalk Image Search system, a tool aimed at helping Smalltalk developers find any string within their current image, such as a literal string.

Exhibit 8.2   RSS object hierarchy.

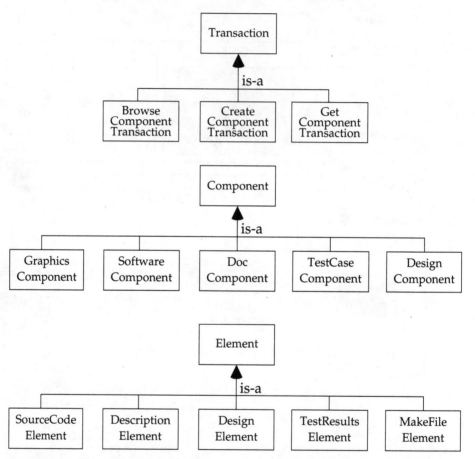

Component Search Engine (CSE) Design
Application Class Mini-Hierarchies

Exhibit 8.6 shows the major components of RSS. RSS includes 66 classes, and 630 methods. It took 23 person-months to complete.

RSS employs the following OO features:

BASIC OO FUNCTIONALITY
- Classes/instances.
- Inheritance/specialization. (maximum five levels deep)
- Methods/messages.
- Virtual methods/polymorphism.

Exhibit 8.3   RSS object hierarchy.

Component Search Engine (CSE) Design
Application Class Mini-Hierarchies (cont)

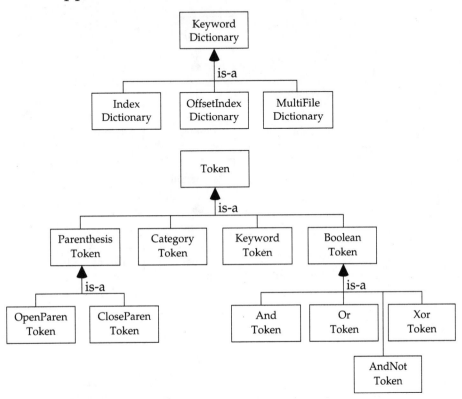

ADVANCED OO FUNCTIONALITY
  – Persistent objects. (ObjectFiler)

DEVELOPMENT ENVIRONMENT
  – Automatic method tracing.
  – Internal class libraries.
  – Editors.
  – Graphical tool for user interface development.

STORAGE MANAGEMENT
  – Repository available.
  – Version control available.

Exhibit 8.4   RSS object hierarchy.

Component Search Engine (CSE) Design Application Class Mini-Hierarchies (cont)

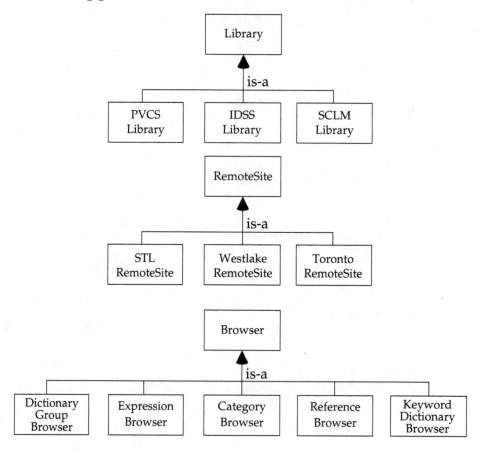

CODE GENERATION
 – Language code generated.
 – Compiled code generated.

PROJECT LIFE CYCLE

RSS was developed in-house at IBM Cary. The development team, managed by Bob Jensen, was made up of Mark Lorenz (technical lead), Bob Brodd, Al Davis, Jeff Kidd, and Janet Kirk.

Exhibit 8.5   RSS reusable components.

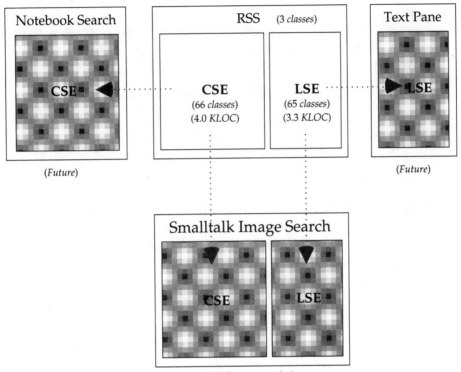

Reuse Support System (RSS) Architecture
Reuse

Exhibit 8.6   System components.

	Hardware	Software
Interface	VGA +	Presentation Manager
Core Code	PS/2 386 +, 8 + MB	OS/2 1.3 +, Smalltalk/V PM 1.4 +
Database	None	None
Development Environment	Lan, 10 + MB, 120 + MB	OS/2, Smalltalk/V PM

Analysis and Design

The Programming Systems Lab at IBM Cary has been involved in object-oriented product development since about 1988.

Requirements were written and verified with users using documents and prototypes.

Some managers were skeptical but accepted the risk of the new technology after being convinced by technical leads.

According to Mark Lorenz:

> Our management relied heavily upon the technical leads to advise them of the best way to meet our goal. We already had experience from previous projects to support our use of object technology. We reused classes from these projects to quickly prototype our proof of concept. This helped gain support for further investment. On each project, it has been important to show continued rapid progress toward our goals. Having a partially developed system to demonstrate the development on an ongoing basis was enormously important.

An extended Wirfs-Brock methodology was used. Those wishing more information on the methodology used can refer to a book written by the project's technical lead, Mark Lorenz, *Object-Oriented Software Development: A Practical Guide*.

Expert systems and structured techniques were considered for this project but rejected in favor of an object-oriented approach.

Again, Mark Lorenz said:

> Our previous successes with object technology led us to use it again. On our original effort in 1988, we were given six months to prove the original concept. The only way we could perceive being able to accomplish this in six months was to use OT, with its benefits, and to do the work in a nontraditional (i.e. not business as usual) way.
>
> We surveyed a number of tools and decided that Smalltalk was the only system that would allow us to focus on the problem at hand. We were afraid that we would use our entire six months working on the scaffolding, tools, etc., and would go out of business unless we took this route. We then cloistered ourselves from day-to-day activities, brought in two consultants who were experienced in OT, and delivered an unheard-of amount of end-user function in that six months. This provided a lot of support for further investment. This original project has resulted in a number of spin-off projects that have been delivering products using OT.

Development

Development required 30 person-months. This worked out to seven person-days per class without formal test and documentation.

Deployment

Users were given an install document, on-line help, and mentoring (expert assistance to get started). This was not unique to the technology.

Performance: The following numbers were the results from running RSS against the lab's entire C code base. The lab has around 850 people, coding primarily in C and a variant of PL/I. The following numbers are based on the C code dictionary. The PL/I dictionary is similar in size. Other dictionaries, such as assembler and Smalltalk code, are smaller. Note that dictionaries can be used for any textual data, such as documentation, and not just for code.

- Source Code Base

    The administrative background task to build the lab's C code dictionary took around 19 hours to run on the mainframe. The source is 221.4 MB, contained in over 5500 individual files. The keyword dictionary is 18.5 MB (8% of the original data) and, with no filtering of noise words, contains over 163,000 keywords. This is what the performance numbers in this section were run against.

    The following RSS expressions were run. In each case, the numbers shown are to find all the references and bring up a window with the component names listed.
    - "sorting" 9.72 seconds, 62 hits
    - "evaluate" 5.58 seconds, 12 hits
    - "strtok" 12.29 seconds, 85 hits
    - "sort and (hash or tree)" 11.46 seconds, 22 hits. This expression involves three keyword lookups, followed by two boolean set logic actions to get the final set of components that satisfy the expression.
    - "(sorting and hashing) and NLS" 25.01 seconds, 28 hits

    Compare this to the average response from running a "grep-like" tool to find single words in a set of files. The following searches were run against 3.3 MB, contained in 529 files in one High Performance File System Directory.
    - "sorting" 174 seconds, 1 hit
    - "the" 126 seconds, 199 hits

    This is one order of magnitude less number of files and two orders of magnitude less source data, but takes 13 times as long to return a result for a one keyword expression. Complex expressions are not supported.

Maintenance

Maintenance (and second release development) has been relatively easy, largely due to the use of abstractions, encapsulation of self-managing classes, and design for reuse. The application was developed with future reuses in mind. This greatly improved the maintainability and reusability of the software. This would have been difficult without object technology.

BENEFITS

According to Mark Lorenz, the benefits of RSS are considerable:

The capability to effectively and quickly sift through large volumes of reusable components (software, documentation, icons, clip art, spreadsheet templates) is now possible. Our lab alone has millions of lines of product code. Certainly not all of this is reusable, but more and more focus on reuse is occurring over time. And object technology is an enabling technology for reuse, so we expect this need to grow.

We experienced two to three times the volume of code delivered than a traditional project. And the functionality of Smalltalk is five times the functionality of traditional code of similar volume. This is after throwing away numerous classes, often multiple times, during the first release development. So, we have less code volume to maintain, with less coupling across the system.

The major focus was on ease-of-use. The success of this UI has allowed many people to use the tool with minimal training or help, supplemented primarily through on-line help.

CONCLUSIONS

Mark Lorenz has written a book, *Object-Oriented Software Development: A Practical Guide,* (Prentice Hall, 1993). He distills his advice to others in the field in this list:

1. Get OT expertise in-house until you grow your own.

2. Focus on the right objects to model your business. You probably won't find these right away. They won't match your function-oriented model of how your business works.

3. Verify your objects and their responsibilities with your customers. This implies scenario walkthroughs and prototyping.

4. Use an iterative development process. Don't be afraid to throw things away. Schedule multiple iteration efforts on difficult end-user functions.

5. Use small teams. Break larger problems into encapsulated pieces, using contracts between the subsystems to control the architecture.

6. Put your best OO developers on your key classes.

7. Plan for reuse as you go. Think about other ways to use a class, so you don't build it in an ad hoc fashion.

8. Use text-oriented tools for a large part of your effort. Graphics are important and needed, but overemphasized. Textual user and model scenarios and Smalltalk-like model browsers go a long way toward effective, rapid development and reviews.

CHAPTER 9

Application Description

SOFTWARE CONFIGURATION MANAGEMENT SYSTEM

STATEMENT OF THE PROBLEM

The Software Configuration Management (CM) System is concerned with software development and maintenance on a large government mainframe installation at the Landschaftsverband Rheinland (LVR) in Cologne, Germany.

Early in 1991 the LVR already had a software portfolio of 5,000 modules of source code, but one of the development projects underway was supposed to add 2,000 more by the end of 1991. There were fears that the old system for source version management would not be able to cope with the upcoming task, so the new CM system was started in June of that year.

The new CM system had to enable smooth operations between developers, testers and production people despite the volume foreseen. In order to manage this task, the new system had to be able to:

- control several thousand sources and executables;
- control all dependencies between them;
- transport software through stages (development, test, production);
- transport bundles of related sources as packages;
- automatically compile sources when necessary;
- record all information in an easily accessible database;
- help auditors to get a complete picture of what was changed and when.

Smooth operations between developers, testers and production people are essential to avoiding time losses due to endless exception handling. This is achieved by bundling sources into packages, by automatically compiling when necessary, and keeping track of the whole process using a database.

SOLUTION: SOFTWARE CONFIGURATION MANAGEMENT SYSTEM

The CM system manages and controls the process of moving software from development to production through any number of intermediate stages on an IBM 3090 mainframe. CM supports an arbitrary number of projects and for each project an arbitrary number of stages, and all kinds of sources (e.g. COBOL/VS, COBOL II, PL/I, C/370, Job Control, Copybooks, CSP, etc.)

Compilations are automatic. Whenever a COBOL program is passed on into a stage, it is compiled automatically and its components are registered in the database. Whenever a copybook or include-file is passed, the CM system keeps track of all resulting compiles and makes sure that they eventually happen.

Special processing takes place for CSP applications, which typically consist of several hundred CSP members, each one of which may occur in many CSP applications. It is critical to make sure that no two CSP applications contain different versions of any given CSP member. At the same time such a situation must be tolerated for short periods of time. Such exceptions are remembered by the system until resolved.

CM allows bundling of related software changes into so-called "orders." A developer may bundle all changes that are required to fix a bug or to deliver a whole system into one order. When the development work is finished, the developer can pass the whole order on to the next stage. All the sources contained in the order are passed on by the CM, which initiates compiles whenever necessary.

Given the large number of sources and long compile times (for at least some languages) it was not sufficient to record the dependencies in the usual way ("program ABC uses include file XYZ"). Instead, the dependencies had to be maintained on the basis of time versions (program ABC of 4/23/92 9:07 uses include file XYZ of 3/23/92 8:11).

CM was built on an IBM mainframe under MVS and TSO using C/370 and DB2. In the analysis phase OOATool from Object International was used on a Mac. This provided the team with a fast and efficient way of learning "object think" and provided a solid basis for implementation.

The transition from analysis to design was straightforward. Each class became a load module and a DB2 table; each attribute became a column of the table; each object became a row of its class' table; and each method became a function in its class' load module.

Every object ID is unique over all the system. All connections in the database are made using object IDs. Messages are sent to objects using their object IDs as addresses. To reach the goal of global addressability, the central mail mechanism (dispatcher) is responsible for two tasks:

- to generate unique object IDs on request from any class;

- to transport messages to objects and the results back to the sender.

Whenever a method requires a service from another object, it sends a message. This is accomplished by calling the dispatcher, passing the object ID of the receiver, the message, and any needed parameters. The dispatcher then determines which class the receiver object ID belongs to and calls that class' load module. The load module contains one long case statement that activates, based on the message, the function that implements the method. The result is passed back to the sender in the C-struct that carried the parameters. Note that the sender does not need to know the class of the receiving object, nor even the machine it resides on.

In effect the principle of persistent data has been put the other way around: the database is no longer a vehicle to make a program's storage persistent. Instead the functions have become a vehicle to make the database objects come alive. An object can respond to a message at any time; there is no activation or deactivation visible to users of an object's services.

Users of the Software Configuration Management System have to understand the concept of environments that software has to pass through on its way from development to production (see Exhibit 9.1.) The environments are connected by mailboxes that each environment's team puts its results in. The team responsible for the receiving environment can then pick up the software bundles, called change orders, from its in-box. In this way each team is in full control of its environment.

In addition to the automatic process support offered by the Software Configuration Management System, each team keeps a manual log that covers all the events observed around the automatic system such as phone calls and pieces of paper that require signatures or cannot be automated yet.

Exhibit 9.2 lists the major components of the Configuration Management System. CM is made up of 20 classes, 600 methods, and 40,000 lines of code.

CM contains the following OO features:

BASIC OO FUNCTIONALITY
- Classes/instances.
- Inheritance/specialization.
    ("Inheritance did not seem to be an important issue in the application domain our project was engaged with. But we now implement inheritance too because we want to use our system in other application areas.")

Exhibit 9.1   Software environments.

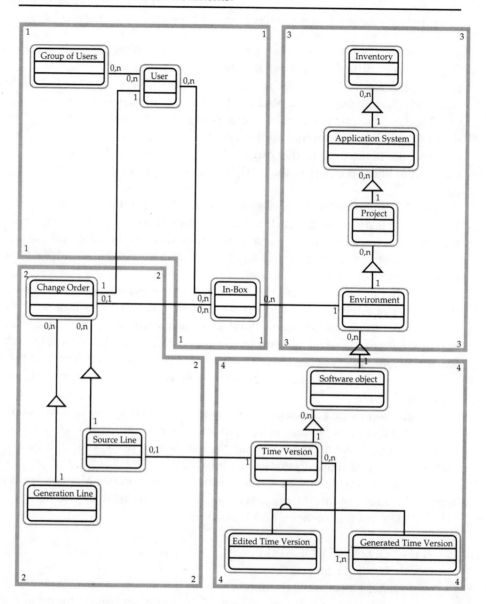

Exhibit 9.2   System components.

	Hardware	*Software*
Interface	3270 terminals	TSO/ISPF
Core Code	IBM Mainframe	C/370
Database	IBM Mainframe	DB2
Development Environment	IBM Mainframe, PC for analysis and design	OOATOOL (Coad/McKenna)

     – Methods/messages. Messages are implemented as sub-program calls as in C++.

     – Polymorphism.

ADVANCED OO FUNCTIONALITY

     – Persistent objects.

        ("Message passing is always possible between all objects in the system!!")

DEVELOPMENT ENVIRONMENT

     – Editors. ISPF/PDF on the mainframe.

STORAGE MANAGEMENT

     – Repository available. (Limited)

     – Version control available. (Version control is the heart of the project.

PROJECT LIFE CYCLE

Analysis and Design

CM was the first OO development project at LVR, but given the circumstances it was an easy sale. According to project manager, Hermann Schmitt:

> We were lucky to get much help from IBM, involuntarily. It helped us a lot to see how much object-orientation their developers had already implemented in AD/Cycle's Repository Manager/MVS (a product dropped in July, 1992). Some of the key people at Landschaftsverband had already taken a thorough look at OO and knew its benefits. In addition, there was a change in the DP department's management. One of the new managers' first questions was "Why should we invest that much money in a dying technology (i.e., the mainframe)?" So obviously, we didn't have to fight much ignorance or resistance. The only concern was: "Can it really be done?" and "Seems too easy to be true."

Analysis followed the Coad/Yourdon methodology. According to Schmitt it really made things easy.

> We think we were in an ideal position when we started with OOA:
> 1. We knew what we wanted
> 2. We had a consultant in the team, who knew software configuration management inside out (M. Roesch).
> The only thing lacking was a suitable documentation tool that would help us to organize all of our thinking without adding too much complexity of its own.

The team also considered a conventional CASE approach, Excelerator from Intersolv (formerly Index Technology). They tried to get a handle on the analysis with Excelerator, but didn't get anywhere. After about two weeks they gave up and decided to try OOATool.

Schmitt sees only benefits of OO in this phase:

> It was our experience that software configuration management, a rather complex topic, could not only be modelled with OOA, but also became simpler by documenting it in an object-oriented way. Of course, this was not due to magic. The reason was simple: By applying the principles of the OOA method of Coad/Yourdon, our thinking became "object-think", something quite natural to humans (only DP professionals seem to have reservations against it).

Development

Starting from their OOA model they used the attributes and connections of the classes to define SQL tables for the DB2 database system and to collect the services of each of the classes in a C/370 module.

For the user interface they used ISPF. The translation was straightforward. The only difficulty they faced the limitations of the mainframe software world: limited compiler, old operating system, important system calls only reachable through assembly subprograms, no-good debugging tools, etc.

Two employees of the Landschaftsverband Rheinland and up to four employees of Roesch Consulting did the actual development, which was completed six months from the start of the design phase. Since the first deployment of the system they have kept adding new functionality in incremental development rounds, each lasting two to three months. The original development effort was about 2,000 person-hours.

Concerning the development software they didn't have much choice. The relational database system DB2 was the only database system that could be employed. As programming languages essentially COBOL and C were available. The architecture of the configuration management system made it necessary to call programs recursively, a feature not available in COBOL. Therefore they had to use C. But the IBM C/370 compiler is rather limited. Using REXX or CLIST was not considered, since these two are interpreted. They would not have been able to handle the load on the mainframe. If it had not been the mainframe, they would have decided in favor of an interpreted language. But the mainframe has only one CPU—or a few—for hundreds of users.

There was a challenge in the middle of development, when they found that the amount of new software would not be 40% of what they already had, but another 200% on top of their existing portfolio of 5,000 applications. This did not only mean a higher volume to be handled but also required changes in the way the system worked, forcing them to go back to OOA to account for the changes. This detour cost only two weeks, because the other parts of the system remained stable. They attribute this to the early decision to implement self-managing objects. This way the impact of the change was reduced to just two classes that had to be reworked.

Schmitt cites other development considerations:

> Macrogeneration is a must. We had only 20 classes, but the methods for these classes showed so much commonality that we felt handcoding them was a waste of time. We are looking at ways to implement this generation capability. A first approach with the M4 generator on the NeXT computer failed because of inadequate mainframe connectivity.
>
> We will try to use FoxPro system's strong generation facilities which allow access to databases in the generation process. It will run on MS-DOS or in the DOS box of OS/2.
>
> The benefits of OO in development came from the strong isolation of the object classes so we could concentrate on the most important classes, first building just stubs of the less important ones. When the less important classes were refined later, this did not disturb the already finished objects. The only drawback was that quite a lot of new ground had to be covered, since there was absolutely no experience we could build on. So we took some curves that proved unnecessary afterwards.

Deployment

Some technical people just couldn't believe that OO could be possible on an IBM mainframe. At first they doubted the possibility of the approach altogether. Later, when the software worked and there couldn't be any doubt about its working, the acceptance issues turned to performance questions. But the team is working on it and we have discovered a significant degree of optimization potential that would not be available to conventional approaches.

The programs were found to be reliable from the beginning. The system could be deployed incrementally with the most important classes being deployed first with full functionality. Other less important classes were deployed with limited capabilities at first, and were completed only later. The re-work of the less important classes had no effect on the classes already in production.

Maintenance

Maintenance of CM is performed by two employees of the Landschaftsverband and one person from Roesch Consulting, all part time. Schmitt makes no distinction between maintenance and incremental development. There are cycles of about two to three months that incorporate all the changes necessary, both errors resolved and new functionality added.

> We don't consider maintenance a problem. The object structure developed in OOA has not changed yet, so changes have no far-reaching consequences. Our objects seem to be really self-managing, so all changes have only local effects. We feel that object technology has delivered on its promise: more stable systems and less ripple effects in the maintenance phase.

BENEFITS

The principal benefit of CM was that a huge workload that was facing the DP operations staff could be handled smoothly. The workload was created by another development project for one of the Landschaftsverband's clients by an independent contractor. This other project was behind schedule and there was some fear that some of the blame could be shifted to the Landschaftsverband's own personnel, if there were any problems when the new project was handed over to production with the new Software Configuration Management System.

As it turned out, the new Software Configuration System was able to handle about 10,000 new pieces of software and about 500 change orders since its introduction. Each change order consisted of about 10 new versions for some pieces of software. From start to finish a change needed about three days from quality assurance to production. The system is now being extended to handle all production turnovers by all developers.

The main benefit of using OO techniques was the amount of functionality that was achievable given the constraints on time and money. Also attributable to OO technology is the fact that the system was put into production on time despite a major change in the requirements in the middle of the five-month development cycle.

Other benefits seen by Schmitt:

From the consulting company involved, Roesch Consulting, we heard that a similar project they were involved in and that was built using conventional methods and tools did cost about 20 times as much, while at the same time providing less functionality in critical areas.

We feel we have in fact implemented an incremental development style. New developments are incorporated based on user demand. As yet there have been no shakeups of our original class structure that evolved from our first OOA effort. Maintenance has been reduced to adding attributes to classes and to changing or adding methods.

Users do not see the difference directly. Nowhere at the surface is it possible to see the object implementation technique.

Since we didn't design the user interface first, but instead let the individual objects handle their own terminal I/O, the resulting dialog capabilities of the system go beyond what could have been planned beforehand. In effect, the user can "walk around" the object world, following any connections the objects/classes have. If there is anything an object needs to know from a user, it just pops up a window asking for the required information.

CONCLUSIONS

Schmitt has pointed advice for others contemplating OO development for mainframes:

Do it. Don't wait. The ORB (Object Management Group's Common Object Request Broker Architecture—CORBA) may be your smooth way out of the IBM mainframe. This is especially interesting, now that IBM seems to have given up the mainframe. Remember: the mainframe-based Repository Manager/MVS, the would-be centerpiece of mainframe-centered application development framework (AD/Cycle) has been dropped by IBM and there are no indications that there will be any significant development tools for the mainframe offered by anyone.

The lack of OO tools and languages in the mainframe environment is no serious obstacle against doing OO on the mainframe. On the contrary, we feel that our architecture, that resembles OMG's CORBA pretty much, might have suffered, if we had viewed OO through the eyes of one of today's popular object-oriented languages like C++ or Smalltalk. It is our belief that the availability of an OO language would have detracted our attention from the more important issues such as active objects and global reachability through systemwide object IDs.

Because of the lack of OO languages we felt free to build a truly object-oriented system. With an OO language we might have ended up with programs which are object-oriented internally, but with a system that would have been function-oriented with passive data and all the problems that are so well known for years. The object-oriented language is not the most important issue, but the ability to store objects persistently and the object-orientation of the whole system and the capability that any object may call any other object at any time. This is supported by the ORB which will work with any language. It is not dependent on C++. In fact, its first language binding has been defined for C, not for C++. Additionally, the main feature of the ORB is message passing between all objects in the system.

CHAPTER 10

Application Description

PROBE: A TOOL FOR COBOL APPLICATION REFINEMENT

Micro Focus Inc., a Silicon Valley software vendor, has used object-oriented technology to build an enhancement to its Micro Focus Workbench product. PROBE: A Tool for COBOL Application Refinement, as the enhancement is called, helps systems analysts fine-tune existing COBOL applications to make the most efficient use of mainframe resources.

STATEMENT OF THE PROBLEM

After a COBOL application is delivering the desired results, some tuning is usually required to optimize performance. Micro Focus wanted to integrate such a fine-tuning tool into its existing product.

SOLUTION: PROBE

PROBE is a 50.1 kb system that runs on PCs under OS/2. It was developed with Smalltalk V PM on top of existing COBOL code. The goal was to provide a system that:

1. Displays, in a highly graphical format, the system resource being used by the application, and
2. Displays, in animation at the module level, the interactions of the application with its runtime environment.

Exhibit 10.1 lists PROBE's major components. PROBE was developed in Smalltalk V. It derives its classes from three sources:

- Windows (used for GUI)
- Smalltalk V libraries
- Original Micro Focus subclasses were used (approximately 30)

Exhibit 10.1   System components.

	Hardware	*Software*
Interface	IBM PM or equivalent	Smalltalk V PM
Core Code	IBM PC or equivalent	Micro Focus COBOL Workbench
Database	N/A	N/A
Development Environment	IBM PC or equivalent	Smalltalk V PM Micro Focus COBOL Workbench

Exhibit 10.2 shows the basic architecture of PROBE.

Exhibit 10.3 shows the Common Communications Interface of the Smalltalk Class Hierarchy.

Probe includes the following OO features:

BASIC OO FUNCTIONALITY
    – Classes/instances. (Approximately 30 new subclasses)
    – Inheritance/specialization. (Specialization of both GUI and DDE classes)

Exhibit 10.2   PROBE architecture.

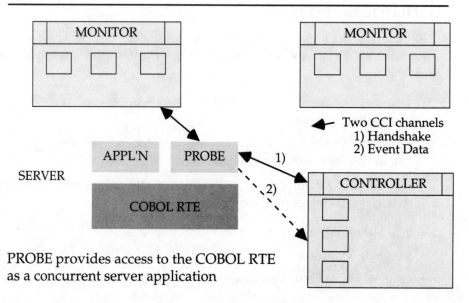

PROBE provides access to the COBOL RTE
as a concurrent server application

Exhibit 10.3   Smalltalk class hierarchy, common communications
interface.

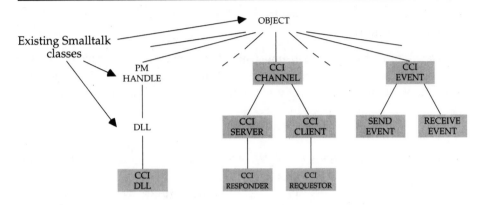

    – Methods/messages.
    – Virtual methods/polymorphism. (Polymorphism heavily used)

DEVELOPMENT ENVIRONMENT
    – Graphical developer interface.
    – Graphical browsers.
    – Automatic method tracing.
    – Internal/external class libraries.

STORAGE MANAGEMENT
    – Version control available.

CODE GENERATION
    – Compiled code generated.

PROJECT LIFE CYCLE

Analysis and Design

Micro Focus considered using object technology because it provided the GUI
necessary, and because it provided for the encapsulation of communication protocols. Other constraints included the need for access to Micro Focus COBOL
runtime environment, and the ability to support asynchronous processing between clients and server.

Key to their choice of OO over conventional approaches was the ability to
reuse the Smalltalk V class library which resulted in major productivity gains.

PROBE was the first OO project undertaken by Micro Focus, but OO technology did not have to be "sold." The design team was made up of Micro Focus

personnel and client representatives. They used Smalltalk V, AM/ST methodology. Alternatives considered: Extension of existing resource monitor.

Development

Development was done in-house at Micro Focus, in six months elapsed time, and required approximately 1,200 person-hours. The software was chosen through research of OO literature and by the reputation of Smalltalk in the market.

Deployment

Integrated with Micro Focus Workbench and deployed in 1991, PROBE is currently used at over 25 client sites.

Exhibit 10.4 shows the client/server use of PROBE. The server is the background window, with two foreground client windows.

Exhibit 10.4   Client/server interface.

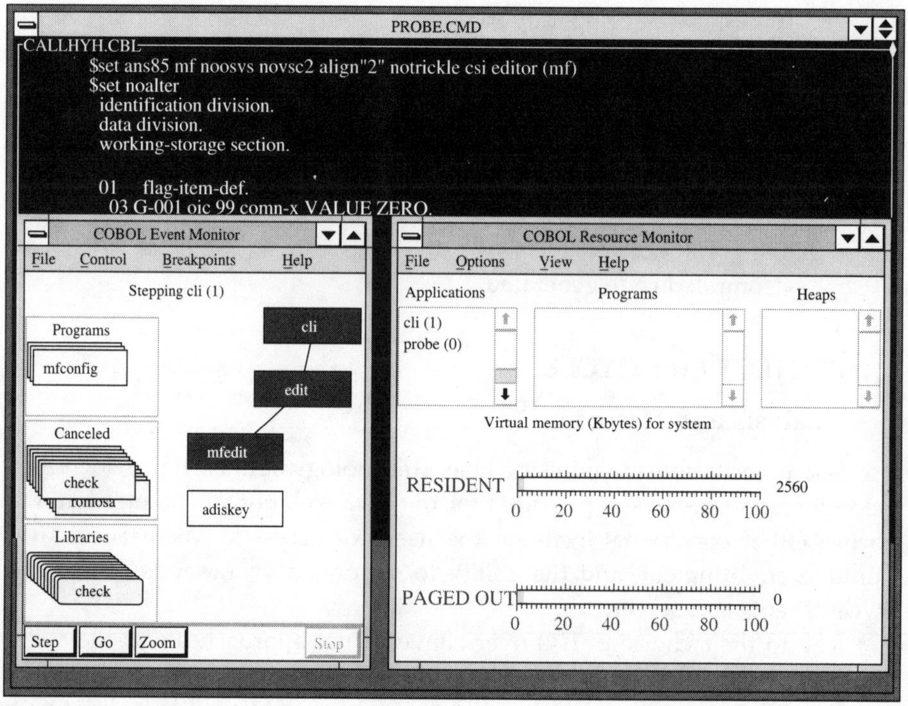

Maintenance

PROBE has been fielded for only nine months, but very little maintenance has been required. To maintain the program, personnel must be familiar with Smalltalk and this is a drawback since there are few such people.

BENEFITS

According to Dan Clarke, PROBE product manager at Micro Focus, a large part of the overall benefit can be attributed to OO.

CONCLUSIONS

According to Clarke:

OO technology has real payoff in terms of reuse and productivity. We are now marketing our own OO development tool. Major gains will be realized in the corporate MIS arena with incorporation of object technology, but these gains require a solid commitment to this technology—and its supporting infrastructures—on the part of the MIS management team.

CHAPTER 11

Application Description

FORMKIT

STATEMENT OF THE PROBLEM

The problem confronting Ross Yakulis, Manager of Information Technology at NeXT Computer, Inc., was twofold:

- Minimize the use of paper forms by substituting electronic forms;
- Put the burden of creation and maintenance of electronic forms on the actual users of the forms.

> When I first arrived at NeXT, the purchase requisition form was a Lotus 1-2-3 spreadsheet and all other forms were on paper. I initially created a simple NeXTSTEP application that was an electronic purchase requisition form to replace the spreadsheet. This electronic form was very popular and I was asked to create a TimeOff form and Check Request form, which I quickly did by copying and changing the first form. These forms were also popular and I was soon overwhelmed with requests to create new electronic forms and to change existing ones. At this point, I knew that unless I got the form requesters to create and maintain their own forms, I was doomed to be "Mr. Electronic Forms" and never do anything else. So I said "No" to all new forms and form changes and proceeded to create the FormKit.

An application such as FormKit would not only reduce paper-waste and move forms more quickly through the process, but also would provide the ability to track a form's progress.

SOLUTION: FORMKIT

FormKit is a collection of objects that, when combined in an appropriate manner, produce electronic form applications without coding. The basic FormKit is six palettes of objects that provide various form functions, a form application object, a form window object, and a tracking application.

Palettes/Objects

Authorization
Provides for form authorization based on UNIX login and password.
Also allows for privileged user override.

Tracking
Assigns sequence numbers to forms and logs form state-changes to a data-base.

MatrixPlus
Provides for math, tabbing, and value assistance/validation, and field copy
(data entered on one window appears on other designated windows.

Calendar
Graphical date picker.

UserName
Defaults requester name to logged-in user.

TexFieldPlus
Provides rich field formatting, validation, and user-customizable error mes-sages.

FileIcon
Allows users to drag attachments onto a form and have the attachment
become part of the form in a compound document.

FormApplication
Provides for the basic document management of open, save, new, print,
dirty document, and overall coordinator of form activity.

FormWindow
Works together with FormApplication and is chiefly responsible for iden-tifying objects on the window.

WhereIsMyForm
This is a tracking application that reports on the status of a form. Was it
approved? Who has looked at the form? etc.

To create a form, the user employs InterfaceBuilder and a generic form tem-plate that has a few things already set up. Users add objects to the form window, create additional windows and so on. When the form is complete the user enters a "make" command from a terminal window and an application is created. The finished application is a fully functioning NeXTSTEP application. A skilled user can create additional palettes for their form or add supplemental behavior to the form by creating a custom object. However, this is rarely needed because the basic FormKit serves most users' needs.

FormKit is an enhancement of existing software, NeXT's NeXTSTEP Application Kit. Exhibit 11.1 shows the classes in NeXTSTEP 3.0, with the new classes created for FormKit in bold.

Exhibit 11.2 lists FormKit's major components.

FormKit includes the following OO features:

Exhibit 11.1 NeXTSTEP object hierarchy.

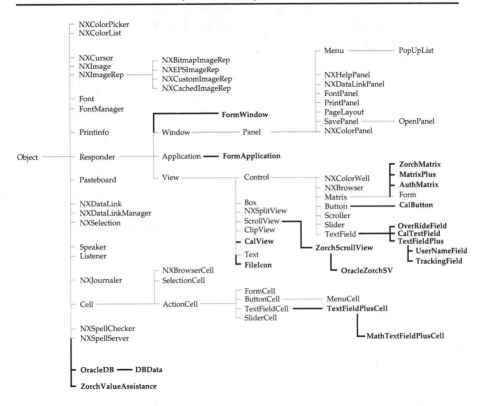

Exhibit 11.2 System components.

	Hardware	Software
Interface	NeXT	NeXTSTEP
Core Code	NeXT	NeXTSTEP AppKit
Database	NeXT	Oracle
Development Environment	NeXT	NeXTSTEP (Objective C and InterfaceBuilder)

BASIC OO FUNCTIONALITY
- Classes/instances.
- Inheritance/specialization.

DEVELOPMENT ENVIRONMENT
- Graphical developer interface.
- Graphical browsers.
- Internal/external class libraries.
- Editors (ProjectBuilder and InterfaceBuilder)
- Graphical tool for user interface development.
- Version control available.

CODE GENERATION
- Compiled code generated.

PROJECT LIFE CYCLE

Analysis and Design

The key requirement calling for an object-oriented approach was the issue of extensibility. Yakulis wanted the forms to be extensible by users who possessed a greater set of skills. The FormKit contains a standard set of "form objects" that cover roughly 90% of electronic forms. By using OO technology, someone wanting to create a form that did something extraordinary could use the FormKit to get 90% of the form complete and easily add the 10% custom portion, or create a new form object to be added to the standard set of form objects. Conventional programming environments are fairly closed systems, and not readily extended by persons other than the creator.

Development

To develop FormKit, common characteristics of forms were distilled from the existing forms and embellished. Objects like pop-up calendar, value assistance object, etc., were placed on loadable InterfaceBuilder palettes, which in turn are used in the creation of forms. A "headstart" nib (NeXT InterfaceBuilder) file was created with standard menus, the FormApplications and FormWindow objects were put in place in the nib file.

The total effort took about three months with two of the months devoted to writing detailed design documentation. FormKit contains approximately 4,000 lines of code.

Deployment

All users requesting new electronic forms, and all managers were sent a mail message announcing the existence of FormKit. Walk-through documentation was provided. As users began using FormKit, Yakulis provided support by answering questions and supplying help when needed. User response was enthusiastic.

Exhibit 11.3 shows a typical screen during the form creation process and depicts the InterfaceBuilder being used to connect together objects in the user interface and to specify the objects' graphical attributes. On the far right is Workspace dock. Going to the left, top to bottom are the InterfaceBuilder object palette, and object Inspector, the form's window, InterfaceBuilder's menu, the form's menu, and InterfaceBuilder's file window.

Maintenance

According to Yakulis:

> Maintenance is the best part of FormKit. All forms are maintained by the form creators and not by IS. IS (me) has only to maintain and enhance FormKit, and not every single form.

Exhibit 11.3   InterfaceBuilder.

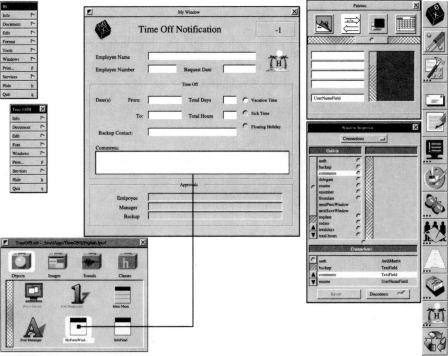

BENEFITS

FormKit has freed the IS department from having to create and maintain countless electronic forms. More than twenty forms have been created with FormKit and are in use at NeXT. IS must only maintain and enhance the basic FormKit. This allows the department to concentrate on new projects that will in turn leverage IS resources.

CONCLUSIONS

According to Yakulis:

> FormKit was a very successful project. It has become an effective sales tool to demonstrate to potential customers the power of OO development. As mentioned earlier, there are now 20+ electronic forms in use at NeXT. The key is to create productivity software to leverage personnel, and push responsibility out to the users.

Domain: Sales and Service

Until recently, computing has been used to automate the backroom operations. Computers and software were too unfriendly to be used with customers. In the 1980s that began to change, and computers have increasingly found their way into the customer service area and into the sales manager's office. Indeed, in the 1990s, one of the major changes in the way that companies do business will stem directly from this new use of computers. The companies that survive and prosper in the late 1990s will be monitoring customers as they make their purchases and service calls, looking for opportunities to improve their products and sales. The real-time networks that these proactive companies will depend on will rely on object-oriented systems that operate in client-server environments. Data will constantly be exchanged to assure that managers have up-to-the-minute information when they make their decisions.

The need for speed, the complexity of the applications, and the network-based nature of these applications will all tend to push sales and service software developers into the forefront of object applications. In fact, as the three applications in this section illustrate, the developers in some leading companies' sales and service computing groups are already there.

United Artists runs 470 movie theaters. In each theater they sell products. To become more effective in their marketing and sales efforts, United Artists has installed a system that tracks sales as they are made throughout their entire network. The system uses a GUI to let marketing managers enter assumptions and ask questions. They might know, for example, that older adults are in certain theaters to see a specific new movie. By observing what is selling and conducting experiments in pricing at certain theaters within the set of those that have older adults, new pricing strategies can be arrived at almost instantaneously. Of all the systems in this book, this system comes the closest to suggesting the kind of business environment in which successful companies will increasingly need to operate if they are to thrive in the near future.

Kash n' Karry has been a major user of object technology. They have explored the development of new OO languages and tools and have created some impressive applications. The Kash n' Karry application described in this section replaces a previous system and significantly enhances its functionality. Using the new application, Kash n' Karry managers are now able to run detailed statistical analysis on lane operator efficiency and peak performance times, and create reports that they could not get in the past.

Alain Pinel Realtors set out to become the most technically sophisticated residential real estate agency in the world. Each agent in their system used a NeXT workstation and a new application suite developed by the company's IS group using NeXTSTEP and Objective C. The graphics are the key to making this system easy enough for computer-illiterate real estate dealers to use without training. Behind the graphics, however, is some very sophisticated programming that allows Alain Pinel agents to get data and organize them in much more effective ways than their competitors do.

CHAPTER 12

Application Description

ALAIN PINEL REALTORS CUSTOM APPLICATION SUITE

STATEMENT OF THE PROBLEM

Alain Pinel Realtors (APR), a Northern California start-up company set itself the goal of becoming the most technically advanced residential real estate agency in the world. By automating the many tedious clerical tasks associated with selling property, Alain Pinel hoped to attract the area's most successful agents and managers and thus dominate the market. Their solution includes significant contributions from object-oriented technology.

SOLUTION: THE CUSTOM APPLICATION SUITE

APR's Custom Application Suite runs on 130 NeXT workstations in the company's two offices. All employees, from managers and agents to clerical personnel, have workstations on their desks, and thus the "Suite" offers an enterprise-wide environment, including:

- Multiple Listing Service interface
- comparative market analysis
- in-house database
- client management
- personal marketing
- message board, in/out board

In conceiving and designing the suite of programs, APR management approached their business as a large interpersonal workgroup, in which a variety of service professionals need to coordinate actions and information in a timely man-

Exhibit 12.1   System components.

	Hardware	Software
Interface	NeXTStation	NeXT Interface Builder
Core Code	NeXTStation	Objective C
Database	NeXTStation	NeXT
Development Environment	NeXTStation	NeXTSTEP, Adamation Tools

ner, both within the company and with related service suppliers (title companies, lenders, mortgage brokers, property inspection services, marketing companies, and publications).

These applications are all based an a common object-oriented tool set and were developed to take advantage of the network environment and unique user-interface capabilities of NeXT computers. All system administration and user training is handled by a single nontechnical employee.

Exhibit 12.1 shows the main components of the Custom Suite.

Exhibit 12.2 shows NeXTSTEP's Object Hierarchy.

Module Descriptions:

1. MLS—Multiple Listing Service Interface

Real estate agents have traditionally accessed regional MLS databases via teletype machines or dumb terminals. Users enter cryptic commands and get printouts of coded property information which they literally cut and paste or retype to prepare presentations for clients. The same tedious procedure is used for entering listings or sales into the MLS for access by others. The process consumes hours and entails considerable clerical work. It uses decade-old technology, is nonintuitive, and forces the same information to be dealt with many times separately. Exhibit 12.2 shows the MLSForms Main form screen.

APR's MLS Interface lets agents fill out a familiar on-screen form to enter listings, report sales, or make searches on various criteria. Many selections are made by clicking on the appropriate options or with pop-up buttons. Multiple MLS systems can be accessed by filling out the data only once. The program then interacts with the MLS computer automatically, freeing the user from tedious data entry. The interface does error checking on entered data and prompts users for missing data for the requested function. Users can observe the flow of commands

Exhibit 12.2   MLSForms main form screen.

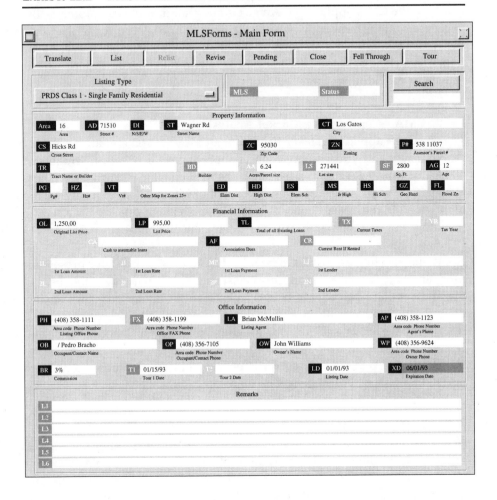

and data exchanged with the MLS, or even revert to traditional command-line interaction, in the MLS Terminal window available on the menu.

APR's MLS Interface automatically reconfigures itself into one of several different screens containing fields for different types of properties on different multiple listing services. It can be customized to fit the exact requirements of any MLS system as the company expands. Users can log onto the MLS by clicking on a single button. The program accesses any available modem over the network, allowing users to share a small number of modems and their respective dedicated phone lines. The program establishes communication and automatically enters the passwords and ID numbers stored in the User Database. Downloaded information can be stored as either a simple log, or as data to be manipulated intelligently in the CMA application. An electronic mail message is automatically sent to all users on the network whenever a listing or sale is reported to the MLS, and the system enters the transaction into the In-House Database. This saves numerous hours reentering data for different functions and making copies for distribution, as well as providing instantaneous updates throughout the company.

2. CMA—Comparative Market Analysis

The CMA application takes data from an MLS session and allows the user to manipulate it easily to prepare reports appropriate for client presentations. The CMA List window contains a list of entries with one line per property. The CMA Detail window provides the complete detail of information on a single property highlighted in the CMA window. This allows agents to quickly browse through inventory to select comparable properties. Exhibit 12.3 shows the CMA List Detail Panel.

While selecting properties to be included in a CMA report for presentation, a user can select and view an appropriate subset of the many available fields from the MLS session. The order of fields can be changed interactively by clicking and dragging the column title bar with the mouse. This also causes the data to be resorted on the left-most field, allowing users to quickly sift through their selection criteria for comparable properties without typing commands. This process, which formerly took up to several hours, can now be completed in minutes and printed out in a professional format with no additional effort.

3. In-House Database

When listings are input to a local real estate board through the MLS application, data is automatically entered into the In-House Database, which contains up-to-the-minute listings for the entire company. Databases from remote sites are linked and updated in real time via dedicated lines. This allows APR to track its business in several significant ways.

Agents can easily browse the company's listings before accessing the MLS, increasing the likelihood of selling both ends of a transaction. This is especially useful for agents "on floor," who are scheduled to answer incoming calls on inventory. All data is available instantly by searching on any field, including name, address, or even comments and ad copy. Management can get instant inventory reports in order to forecast their sales, cash flow, and spot sales trends.

Ad copy, which is entered in MLS Forms during the listing process, can be printed out in a single report by the administrator responsible for placing newspaper ads. This alleviates one of the chronic problems in the business, that of getting ad copy placed on time for publication deadlines.

Exhibit 12.3 CMA list detail panel.

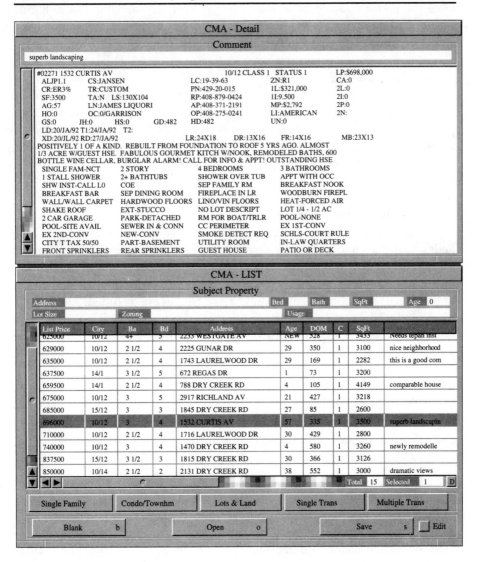

"Open houses" are a key tool in the sale of real estate. Agents sign up for open houses on line, giving easy access to open house schedules. An open house report gives management instant visibility into how many homes are being held open and by which agents. These reports are also handy tools to show clients the level of exposure their property is receiving. A single report shows all advertising and open house activity on a given property.

As in all the modules, the viewable fields and their order are user-definable from the menu and can be changed interactively by clicking and dragging the fields in the main window. This means it can be rearranged interactively to suit each individual user's preferences or sort by different criteria.

4. Who's Calling

Who's Calling is a fully automated client management system commercially available from Adamation. Numerous modifications were made to customize the program to APR's specific requirements. It includes the ability to attach voice messages to client records, and to associate files such as contracts, letters or pictures with a client record, giving users access to all information on a client in one convenient place.

5. Farms (Personal Marketing)

Farms are geographical areas to which agents regularly mail personal marketing materials to develop business. Data files can be entered directly or loaded from Dataquick or Metroscan files, originating in County Tax Assessor records, into APR's Farms application for mailing. Multiple farm files can be merged and duplicates flagged. Both mailing and site addresses are included. All fields can be used for searches to derive lists of names and addresses for mailing. Resulting farm files can be named or sent to mail merge files, mailing labels or printout reports.

6. Message Board, In/Out Board

APR's Message Board and In/Out board are made possible by a sophisticated user tracker, which keeps track of where users are logged in around the network, even at different sites. Users need not be at their regular workstations.

PROJECT LIFE CYCLE

Analysis and Design

Because APR was a start-up, speed of development, along with cost, was the most important factor in designing a system. Its goal was to have the first production system in place within 45 days. As Mark Richards put it:

> We felt we had to move quickly to take the market by storm. As a start-up in a competitive market, we didn't have one to two years to get a system up. We needed powerful networked computers, but we also needed a GUI that was easy to learn and use. Most of our users were completely computer-illiterate.

Initially object-orientation was not of primary concern. The primary concern was to rapidly deploy a system that would be critical to the operation of the company. Research led them to NeXT, which happened to employ object technology throughout. OO did not have to be sold, the rapidity of the development sold itself.

Development

The first decision was to find a consultant who could develop these applications within a very tight time schedule. Adamation, Inc. was chosen because they have demonstrated an ability to develop and deploy custom applications quickly using NeXT computers. Adamation uses the development environment embodied in the NeXTSTEP operating system. Their years of expertise using NeXTSTEP produced a wealth of reusable, tested objects. This preexisting object library was key to rapid development.

The project consumed approximately 1,000 person-hours, and deployed an initial system in 45 days.

Deployment

Each agent and staff member has a NeXT workstation. Three NeXTStations function as servers. Twenty training modules were developed to break the applications into one-hour courses. The courses were taught by administrative staff with no prior computer experience. Users could retake classes at their convenience until comfortable. Two nontechnical staff people split time between training 140 users, system administration, coordinating new software design, and debugging newly delivered modules.

A major benefit of OO in this phase was that user interface problems that turned up could be quickly fixed. User response has been enthusiastic. The agents view the system as a major competitive advantage in their work.

Maintenance

Adamation continues to handle system maintenance and enhancement. Bug fixes and changes take around one-half person months each month from the contractor. This includes changes to the constant stream of new modules. The system has been through three major revisions in the last year, mostly in response to user feedback.

BENEFITS

The benefits of the APR Custom Suite can be measured by the company's enthusiasm. According to Mark Richards:

We have become custom software junkies. We understand deeply how dramatically software tools can affect the productivity, morale, and public identity of an organization. We have stepped up our development efforts and have put numerous new projects in the budget. Custom software tools has become a significant portion of the unique identity our company is building in the market for real estate services.

CONCLUSIONS

Other observations from Richards include:

It is critical to get key personnel involved in the design process—those who know the nuts and bolts of the business best. These are typically people who are very busy and critical to the operation of the company, and are least able to spare the time. Software design must become a priority of these people for an adequate period of time if the applications are to become truly useful to the organization.

Bringing in consultants who had significant experience in large system object-oriented development saved us considerable time and headache. Out team was up to speed instantly and we had our first set of mission-critical applications deployed in 45 days. Any not-invented-here syndrome should be carefully guarded against if this expertise does not exist in-house. Being in an object-oriented environment is especially helpful if you have access to a rich library of well-tested objects and tools. Without these we would have spent considerable time and effort coming up to speed in OO.

CHAPTER 13

Application Description

RETURNS PROCESSING CENTER DAMAGED PROCESSING SYSTEM

Kash n' Karry (KnK), a large retail grocery chain headquartered in Tampa, Florida, has made a major commitment to object technology. Developers at KnK's IS department have created their own object-oriented development tool called "KnK Language," and later enhanced it with a Persistent Object Manager. The application to be described is one of many end-user applications built with KnK Language.

STATEMENT OF THE PROBLEM

In 1987, Kash n' Karry instituted a centralized Returns Processing Center in an effort to recoup lost revenue due to damaged goods. The original processing system was provided by Processor's Unlimited. The system included a Series 1 computer, lane stations, printer and console. Each week, after scanning, a tape was made, FedEx'd to Processor's, reports were run against the data, and printed reports FedEx'd back to the center. There was a monthly charge for the use of the system, plus a percentage based on the costs of the processed goods.

In 1991, Kash n' Karry, in accordance with its "New Architecture Plan," redesigned the entire system. The purpose of replacing the outside vendor with an in-house system was to reduce the costs of return processing and to allow KnK to retain the intrinsic data associated with the processing. The original system provided the processing needs, but only reflected the data processed in report form. With the new system, KnK would be able to run detailed statistical analysis on lane operator efficiency, peak performance times, and run reports not previously available, or available only at extra cost.

The Returns Processing Center was chosen as an excellent pilot/test bed for the Kash n' Karry New Architecture. The New Architecture revolves around fully distributed object computing and the concept of a "simulation" of the business, rather than classical applications. The RPC represented a mini-Kash n' Karry, with stores, vendors, items, warehouses, employees and scanning lanes. It also required substantial transaction rates (30,000 to 50,000 per day). This provided an excellent trial by fire for Kash n' Karry's new object technology.

SOLUTION: RETURNS PROCESSING CENTER DAMAGED PROCESSING SYSTEM

Kash n' Karry's new damaged returns processing system runs on a Sparc II workstation with NCD x-stations and SPECTRAPHYSICS scanners. The system has two main components, the lane operator stations, and supervisory functions.

The lane operator station is made up of an NCD x-station encased in a tower, a SpectraPhysics scanner, and an Intermec label printer. The application run at the lanes is a single screen, which allows the operator to change stores, process goods (UPC key entry or scanning), and associate quantities with the processed goods. Each piece (display, scanner, printer) is controlled by an object, which in turn is made up of many other objects. When a lane operator scans (or enters) a UPC, the data specific to the item is displayed on the screen and a label is printed specifying the warehouse area where the goods should be placed. Exhibit 13.1 shows the lane operator's screen.

The supervisor functions are broken down into maintenance functions and lane control. The maintenance functions provide for the updating of the database regarding stores, operators, and supervisors. The attributes of the items are displayed to the supervisor, and are reflected into the database for immediate use by the lanes. Lane control provides a real-time view of the lane, and allows a supervisor to enable/disable lane functions. When instantiated, the lane control object requests a connection of the lane, and then becomes a view of lane operations as shown in Exhibit 13.2. Current lane operator, login time, number of scans and units processed are updated at every state change of the lane. The lane is aware of all views connected to it and notifies them at every state change. If the view determines that the state change is pertinent to its views, it will request the information it needs and display that information. Consistent with the "New Architecture Plan," these views can be executed from any machine in the network.

The final piece of the system is the reporting mechanism. Reports are written in ESQL and are run on a week and period (monthly) basis, although request reports can be run at any time. The reports automatically feed Wingz spreadsheets for accounting purposes. The reporting was done using third generation technology because the New Architecture tools being developed were not complete by the time the Returns Processing Center's application needed to be in production. Exhibit 13.3 shows RPC's main components.

Exhibit 13.1   Lane operator's screen.

Kash n' Karry
Returns Processing Center

Lane Number: **1**

Mode: **Damaged**

Operator: Buddy   Store: 866

Please Enter UPC   : |

TE

1   Dentyne Cin Gum   01254630130

Set Store	–(F1)
Enter UPC	–(F2)
Quantity–1 tag	–(F3)
Quantity–multiple Tags	–(F4)
Recycle	–(F5)
Backout Item	–(F6)
Logoff	–(F7)

Exhibit 13.2   Lane operations view.

Lane No.	Active	Mode	Operator	Login Time	Total Scans	Total Items
1	☒	Damaged	Buddy	09:03:44	3	50

The Returns Processing Center System was created with a Kash n' Karry proprietary language, called KnK Language.

KnK Language is an expert system that contains the rules for object-oriented development. The expert in this case is the system architect who teaches the system the rules and productions of object-oriented systems.

Written in yacc and lex, this rule-based, object-oriented code generator facilitates formal methodologies, standards, and architectural prototyping. This pro-

Exhibit 13.3   System components.

	Hardware	Software
Interface	NCD X Stations	Interviews Class Library (Stanford), KnK Widgets
Core Code	Sun Sparc 2, 32 mg	C++
Database	Sun 470, 128 mg	KnK Object Manager, Informix
Development Environment	Sun Sparc 2's, 64 mg Sun 670's, 256 mg	Centerline ObjectCenter (C++), KnK Language

vides a means to enforce good design practices while allowing the freedom to change and experiment with different architectural approaches.

The KnK Language inference engine reads in a class specification file and generates C++ source code. Classes and application contexts are expressed through a specification language comprised of keywords and arguments. This specification language is designed to capture the essential information about classes and applications without getting bogged down in the technical details of the target language. The input statements are processed by the inference engine which creates the right "influence" of code.

The rules effect, or "influence," the desired outcome of the definition. This is called "genetic inheritance," which differs from classic inheritance. Instead of inheriting the attributes of one's parents and then extending or hiding the parent attributes, the inference engine selects all or part of the desired parent attributes based on criteria within the class specification, similar to a parent's genes being passed on to its offspring. Genetic inheritance borrows many ideas from Meta Object Protocol, applying them to class architecture design (methodology), not simply the class definitions themselves.

According to Chuck Hill, who along with Tim Thornton, helped write KnK Language:

> By embedding object strategies in the inference engine, the rules of good conduct for an object are invisible to application programmers—they are free to focus on the application, not the syntax. This is a subtle, but key, advantage of the expert system approach: it creates a clear division between the applications and their technical implementation. Without this division, the application programmer would be responsible for such technical schemes as garbage collection and distributed object management. By placing technical implementation within the KnK Language, we are free to change it with no impact on our applications.

Included with KnK Language is a class library of intrinsics including KnK-Object, KnKInteger, KnKMoney, KnKString, KnKFloat, KnKEnum, etc., which provide scalability and portability to applications. These classes handle all operating system and hardware dependencies, in effect creating a virtual machine. For example, this allows objects on 16-bit, 32-bit, etc., machines to provide identical behaviors and to interact with each other with no visibility to the application programmer.

Also included is a class library of KnKWidgets which allow objects to display themselves and negotiate with other objects for presentation space, with optional involvement by the programmer. This has allowed the extension of KnK Language to include an object-knowledgeable report writer.

PROJECT LIFE CYCLE

Analysis and Design

James Stikeleather, Director of Systems Development at Kash n' Karry, described the development process:

> We went through many iterations of trying methodologies known to us from experience or training and were frustrated with the results. It wasn't until we realized that the new paradigm of object-oriented allowed us to MODEL a business activity, rather than just track it, that we began to focus on information and behavior instead of data and process. We eventually evolved to something that resembles CRC cards and actually having developers pretend they are objects in the system and have them role-play the objects as though they were actually the system. This in conjunction with lots of rapidly developed prototypes (straw man, tin man, iron man, steel man, then a production system) did more for clarifying what needed to be produced than any real analysis and design methodology. We are trying to formulate what we do into a methodology and we hope someday someone will develop a methodology that gets the utmost out of object-oriented techniques.

Development

Development took place from September through January with deployment in February. According to Jeff Jones, applications developer:

> There were no traditional phases, just lots of prototypes until the last one was put into production. We now know that we do need a phase to prepare for operational support, but feel this pattern will hold true for all of our development. We should add that there were approximately six months of architecture work that preceded working the RPC problem domain.

Stikeleather continued:

Probably the most important lesson we learned from the exercise of developing the RPC is the importance of an architecture. Actually more time was spent in developing how our objects would behave generically than in the actual problem domain coding of the RPC. We also learned painfully that traditional MIS methods of project management, source code control, and testing were not up to the tasks associated with an object-oriented environment. An object-oriented system with lots of rapid prototypes does not fit the traditional waterfall approach. Also when prototyping, there is no clear delineation as to when one phase of development ends and another begins. Traditional techniques do not account for the work done on an architecture, as point solutions generally address these types of issues within the single piece of monolithic code which is the system. When developing for potential reuse, more time is spent in architecture than in problem domain, at least in the initial systems. Then the added complexity is introduced by coding the problem domain independent of the technical implementation architecture, which may change as we learn more and as technology changes.

Deployment

Again, according to Stikeleather:

Traditional MIS policies, practices and procedures for moving systems into production do not work well in OO. How do you capacity plan when the code is floating around the network at any point in time? How do you test when you are running a simulation where a transaction can have different results based upon the state of the simulation and current simultaneous and previous transactions? These are problems that people developing real-time systems have had to wrestle with, but have not really occured in the business world heretofore. Also, traditional MIS systems are controlling, one screen does one transaction and that is all you can do. Systems developed under OO paradigms tend to be enabling, where from one screen the users can wander the entire simulation and work with whatever catches their fancy. If there is a problem, you can't just test the one transaction, you have to understand the simulation and the business and what the users are trying to accomplish in order to be of help. This is a much more difficult process than a traditional MIS help desk is prepared to handle.

Maintenance

The benefits of developing this system in an object-oriented language have already become apparent. There was a need to change how the labels were to be printed under certain circumstances. The printer object was modified to meet these needs, hooked into the system, and was functional the first time. No other objects were tested, or needed to be.

BENEFITS

RPC met its goal of increasing KnK's control over its return processing and provided increased reporting flexibility and delivered other benefits as well.

The new system also decreased training time, and increased operator efficiency. The original system required about two weeks to get used to and learn the special codes. The new system displays this information in a menu format, highlighting the current selection. Operator efficiency has increased an average of 25%, with a peak of 30%. This has proven to have direct monetary savings. At certain times of the year, the Returns Center has to process so many goods, that a backup occurs. Historically, the double shifts lasted about two weeks, but with the new system, the double shift lasted only one week, and the amount of goods processed was greater.

CONCLUSIONS

The project team has learned much from RPC. According to Stikeleather:

> There are cultural, educational and training issues in using object technology that we underestimated. First, a typical mainframe programmer is not degreed and has a very specialized knowledge set that is more traditional than academic. OO introduces a whole new paradigm for building systems that is difficult to master and understand without a broad exposure to computer science. C++ exacerbates the problem (try explaining a pointer to a COBOL programmer) with technical details above and beyond the OO paradigm. Also, without the broad exposure to computer science concepts, it is difficult to believe or see the benefits of OO technologies and therefore not be enthusiastic about the effort required to learn. We have spent years rewarding programmers for production, generally measured in lines of code. It is a cultural change to get programmers to think in terms of reusability and to reuse already existing objects.
>
> OO requires a developer who is a systems analyst, designer, programmer, quality assurer, and maintenance programmer all in one. We come to the conclusion that there are really three types of jobs, each of which encompasses all of the traditional MIS roles. First there are model builders/prototypers who build simulation models of the problem domain in order to gain understanding of what needs to be done through prototypes. Then there are "lego engineers," people who specialize in building reusable components based upon the models built by the prototypers and who maintain the integrity of the overall "simulation" of the enterprise. And lastly, there are "applications" developers who build the "views" of and into the overall simulation that users interact with.
>
> The biggest surprise to us was the time and effort spent on architecture and reusability. While they have the long-term payback, we did not expect the difficulty in learning how to build a highly reusable object. And to do that we discovered we had to have a well thought out object and business simulation architecture to ensure the objects would truly be plug-and-play lego blocks. We found a 30–40% overhead effort on each object to really make sure it is reusable.

OO represents a genuine paradigm shift, a change in the set of questions we
ask, a change in the world view of those who work in the field, and an inablility
of those who have made the transition to communicate with those who have not.
It is also inevitable.

CHAPTER 14

Application Description

ECIS

STATEMENT OF THE PROBLEM

United Artists' Theatre Circuit Inc. runs 470 movie theaters throughout the United States. The majority of the theaters have multiple screens showing concurrent films and thereby attract different audiences with their associated concessions preferences. Contract obligations with motion picture distributors are based on a percentage of admissions collected, with the percentage being as high as 70% in the initial weeks of a film. Profits, therefore, rely on the efficient sale of concessions during the brief time that the theater-goer is in the lobby prior to the start of the feature. What was needed was the ability to generate maximum yields from concession sales.

Further, the theater business is highly competitive and dominated by five major players. To compete and grow requires the ability to "drive" business parameters in a real-time fashion. The goal was to institute a revenue enhancement and yield management concept that previously had been used primarily by the airline industry.

SOLUTION: ECIS

The Executive Concession Information System (ECIS), was developed to become the foundation of a comprehensive revenue enhancement and yield management system. The first element of the system is the ability to quickly analyze concession sales utilizing a variety of parameters. This foundation ultimately delivers the ability to dynamically adjust concession pricing and availability based on target audience. Prior to this system, information necessary for this kind of decision making was laboriously gathered, manually entered into spreadsheets, hand massaged, and ultimately delivered as a report. Each question prompted the delivery of a tedious "one of" solution without consistency. The preparation of reports relied on individuals with unique knowledge on where data resided, its format, and how to interpret it. ECIS provides a consistent system for gathering, managing, interpreting, and presenting information. This provides the people asking the questions with direct access to the information, rather than keeping it the sole domain of assistants and analysts.

ECIS had to address the needs of a variety of users who monitor sales from different perspectives. Users include the CEO and President, who needed high-level overviews, the CFO, and various VPs whose responsibilities include concessions, film buying, and marketing. The system needed the flexibility of SQL (the ability to construct complex retrieval requests) while removing its crypticism.

ECIS is comprised of several components, each accessible through large buttons at the bottom of the screen. Users simply select a date range by clicking on a beginning and end button. A month-at-a-glance calendar is presented. Clicking on a day sets the appropriate date range.

The first part of ECIS is accessed by clicking on a button which has a color-coded map of divisions as an icon. This presents the "32,000 ft. view." The user is presented a map showing four theater divisions. Four windows display total sales, attendance, and per capita revenue corresponding to each division for the selected timeframe. Users can drill down by clicking on the desired region of the map. This action zooms the user into the district. The processes can be repeated several times until ultimately detailed concession sales for an individual theater is displayed. Exhibit 14.1 shows the summary view of concession sales.

Exhibit 14.1   Summary view.

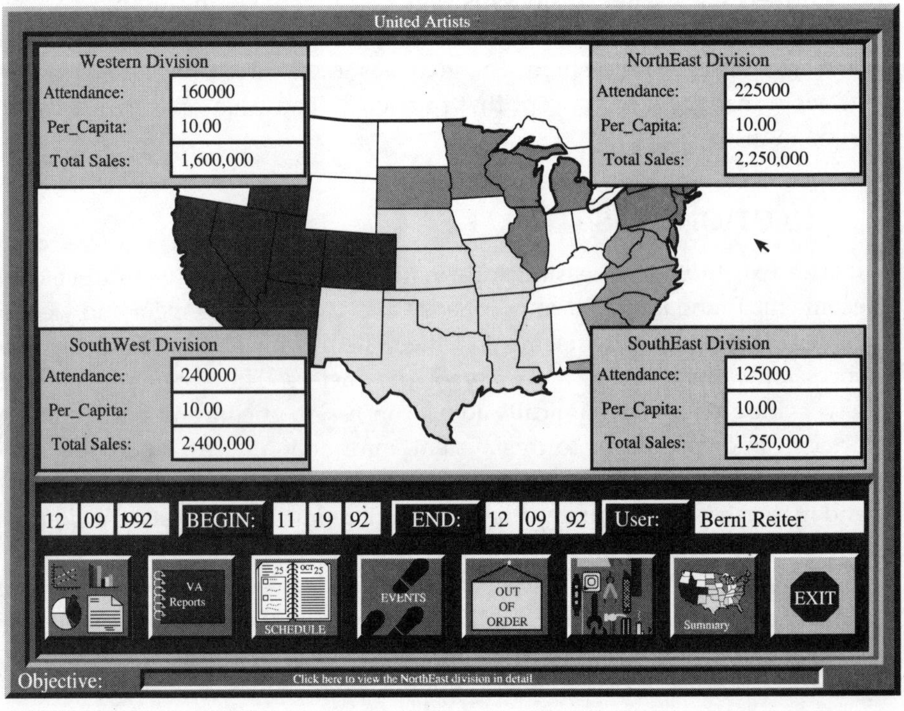

A tools button allows users to create named sets. For instance, a user may want to monitor Butterfinger sales in a college test market. Out of nearly 500 theaters, which ones constitute a college market? The set option allows the users to: select a category (e.g., theater, product, location), select individual items moving the entry into the set window (e.g., college market = Boulder, Fort Collins, Tempe, etc.), and name the set. These sets can be used in the inquiry construction section of the systems in the formulation of retrieval requests (e.g., select Butterfinger concession sales for the specified date range where set is "college market").

By pointing and clicking, users construct their own ad hoc retrievals, analysis, and output specifications. Behind the scenes the application is generating, in many cases, 50-line SQL statements for execution.

The user interface uses a concept of "work order" for requests. Users are presented with a spiral notebook with six tabs. The first tab allows users to gather general sales information. The user can select: basic math functions, information categories (unit cost, spoilage, revenues, per capita, budget versus actual, etc.), groupings (by division, district, circuit, theater, time period, etc.), and an output format (pie chart, line graph, bar, report). Each button is responsible for constructing an SQL phrase which is later assembled and submitted to a server for processing. Exhibit 14.2 illustrates the creation of a work order.

Exhibit 14.2   Work order creation.

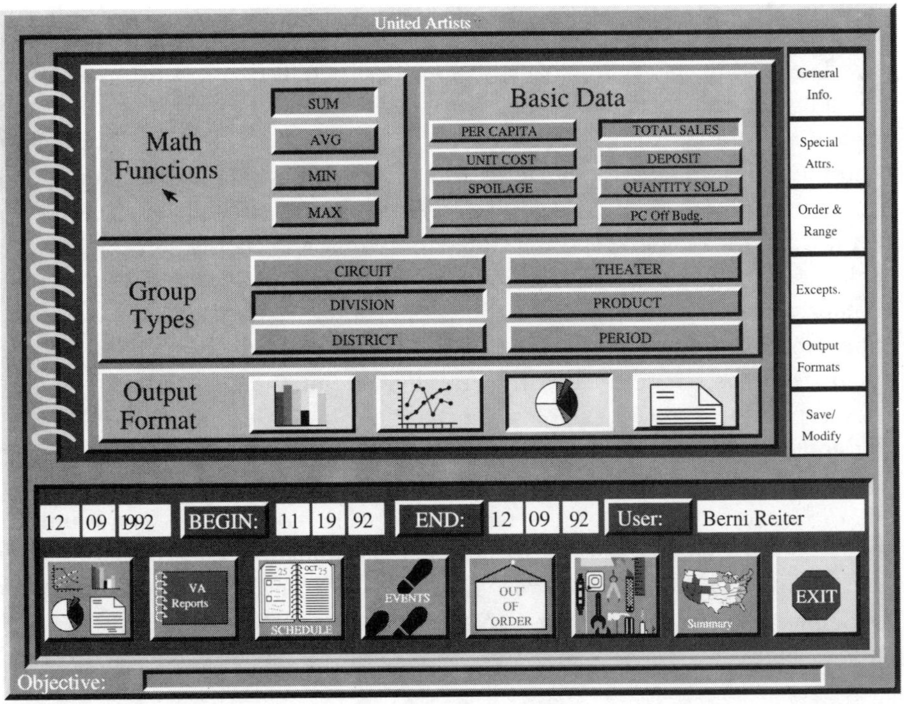

Exhibit 14.3   Selection results.

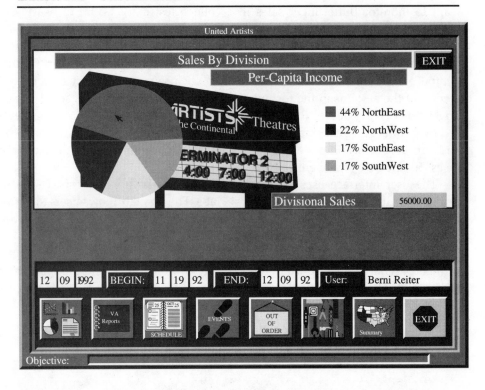

The top four tabs allow users to specify different facets of the inquiry, which include general information, detailed specification, ordering and ranging, and exception criteria. Additional tabs allow users to specify detailed output formats and the ability to save the retrieval and output specifications by name for subsequent execution. Exhibit 14.3 shows an example of the results of a selection.

ECIS uses a client/server architecture with DOS clients and a UNIX server. Sales information was imported from a Prime system and loaded into a Sybase database residing on the server. The application was written in MacroScope, a non-procedural English-like development language which includes libraries of pre-existing objects coupled with a graphical point-and-click CASE tool allowing developers to "draw" the application and have the code generated automatically. Exhibit 14.4 shows the main components of ECIS.

A 4GL tool, MacroScope encompasses a "staff" of computer-science objects that manage the details of interfacing with technologies (GUI, communications, math and modeling, database access, data manipulation, etc.). Each object on the staff is assigned a unique job responsibility. An object's associated functionality is defined as messages or scripts to MacroScope system level objects.

Exhibit 14.4 System components.

	Hardware	Software
Interface	PC Client, HP Server, later 486 based server, Ethernet LAN	MacroScope
Core Code	PC Client, HP Server, Ethernet LAN	MacroScope
Database	PC Client, HP Server, Ethernet LAN	MacroScope (client and server), and Sybase server, then Watcom
Development Environment	PC Client, HP Server, Ethernet LAN	MacroScope "5GL" development environment

For example, clicking on a business graphics icon invokes the dialogue which orders the formatting object to assemble the individual SQL phrases which have been held in memory into a complete SQL statement. A message to the Sybase object to execute the statement follows. The Sybase object is responsible for network interface and interaction between the client workstation and server SQL engine.

MacroScope is sold by Objective Systems, Inc., of Boulder Colorado.

PROJECT LIFE CYCLE

Analysis and Design

The ECIS grew from the need to recover some portion of the loss due to improper inventory levels, spoilage, employee theft, employee consumption, and other factors. Gradually the focus shifted to revenue and profit yield enhancement. Initial design team members included executive users, IS, and Objective Systems, Inc.

United Artists evaluated client/server architectures, graphical user interfaces, relational databases, etc., and also had experience with conventional 4th generation languages promoted by database vendors. 4GLs allow users to quickly create adhoc reports and construct simple interactive transactions. Their output formats are based on terminal screens (e.g. 80 characters by 24 lines) or printers (typically 132 characters per line). 4GLs do not deliver the kind of graphical interfaces and output formats that PC client workstations are capable of producing. What was mandatory was to let users construct their own inquiries, analysis, and subsequent output formats. The system needed to accommodate a wide variety of users and business interests and to allow flexibility in accessing sales information in any way possible, with tens of thousands of reporting and graphing options.

Development

The initial development effort required approximately 600 person hours and lasted six weeks, two weeks for design and four weeks for implementation.

Deployment

Deployment of ECIS was relatively simple. Some of the end users had participated in the design, and so were already familiar with the system. Other users were given a high level presentation, and then were asked to test drive the system until they felt comfortable with it.

This ease of deployment was made possible by the intuitive and obvious nature of the interface and the dynamic help feature described above.

Maintenance

One of the features of MacroScope is the maintainability of its applications by non-IS client staff. The application is described in concise message scripts. The average number of messages per object within ECIS is 25. MacroScope enforces modularity (encapsulation), making it easy to locate code requiring modification. Maintenance of ECIS is currently being performed by United Artists.

BENEFITS

Speed of development with short term ROIs is the principle benefit stressed by Berni Reiter, of Objective Systems, Inc.:

> Reuse of object libraries has changed the expectations of software development. Projects that used to require years, can now be implemented in weeks. This provides the ability to solve today's problems today, rather than solving today's problems, say, two years from now. The latter typically delivers sub-optimal solutions which, while solving problems identified two years ago, do not address new and changing issues.

CONCLUSIONS

When asked what advice she'd give those contemplating an OO development effort, Ms. Reiter extolled OO tools, such as her company's MacroScope, for rapid development.

As a result of implementing ECIS using object-oriented techniques, a key development concept became apparent: Traditional object-oriented views have concentrated on a noun and adjective type philosophy. What became evident was that the primary object to be implemented was not a Concession Object, but rather the objects were the *verbs* associated with the management of the business. It is these business processes that offer maximum reusability

The first layer of object reusability needs to be in accessing technologies. A tremendous amount of software has been written in which developers program and reprogram the same code over and over for every application. For example, say the application needs to interface with a database manager. The developer first needs to open the database by coding "call dbopen using . . .". Following the open request are pages of error handling logic "if condition code is equal to. . . ." This code is typically written over and over, sometimes incompletely or inconsistently. Some technologies are easier to integrate than others. For example, HLLAPI which facilitates 327x emulation with IBM mainframes, is comprised of 57 separate procedures. Using MS Windows for delivering graphical user interfaces is comprised of over 550 procedures. MacroScope hides the interfaces to technologies and associated error handling.

Boyd J. Inman, Senior VP for Information Services at United Artists' Theatre Circuit has formed a number of conclusions as a result of the ECIS project:

In addition to the aforementioned knowledge acquired from the project, it has also been accepted that the software "verbs" are disposable. The need or desire or fear associated with growing, maintaining and continuing to use legacy system software is no longer valid. When the business changes and needs change, replace the "verbs" and go on.

Another facet is the reusability of the code. It would seem that executive management, middle management, and some non-management personnel view their business responsibilities from consistent points of view within their job framework. For example, the theatre president looks at national, divisional, district, theatre, etc., the same way for concession sales, inventory flow, margins, cash gain, etc. The drill down code, philosophy, and therefore the "verbs," are reusable for all because they view the business the same way.

It is my advice that others should step back and view the necessary "verbs" required for the development process in the same way the user sees the business. Do not fall into the trap of viewing the business as your technology expertise dictates. Corporate America will soon insist on returning control of organizations back to the people accountable for the success of the enterprise.

Real object-oriented technology is the tool to right-size IS and deliver results in a timely, cost effective manner.

Domain:
Government and Utilities

All too often, the private sector leads the way toward increased effectiveness and productivity while the public sector appears to wallow in a bureaucratic mire. Given this historical stereotype, it was rewarding to see some solid applications from the public sector. The two summarized in this section illustrate the kinds of results that were achieved.

One Call Concepts, creator of the first application, is actually a private corporation that is retained by utilities to handle calls regarding construction and digging. The idea is simple: by pooling their information at a One Call center, utilities can give a caller all the information required about a particular location while also ensuring that every utility's interests are protected. Implementing this idea, however, is far from simple. All of the location information from the various utilities has to be collated in a single, map-based system. To facilitate this process, One Call developed its Mapping Software Library.

They had a reliable library up and running in just seven months, which set a new productivity record for their developers even though it was their first object-oriented project. The resulting system had fewer defects, is easier to maintain, and runs faster than their previous, non-OO systems. Development of this system also produced a great deal of reusable code: One Call already has five new applications in the works based on the classes developed for their first system.

The Civil Aviation Authority of the United Kingdom developed a highly ambitious application to help it manage the huge amount of information available to its managers. In a software *tour de force*, it created a Business and Management Support System that included four major components:

1. A personal office manager, including electronic Rolodex, calendar, time manager, and list manager

2. A numerical and graphical viewer that works like a spreadsheet and provides information on all the CAA's ongoing operations

3. A project manager that constantly monitors work in process in terms of progress, cost, and vendor performance

4. A human-resource manager that creates and maintains corporate organization charts on screen, allowing navigation throughout the organization and providing ready access to people and projects in each grouping

The total elapsed time for this project, including analysis, design and development, was two months.

CHAPTER 15

Application Description

MAPPING SOFTWARE LIBRARY

One Call Concepts, Inc. is a ten year old Laurel, Maryland firm that manages and operates public utility "one call" centers for many states. One Call centers are set up by state utility boards to handle calls regarding construction and digging, and to notify any utility which may have facilities which are threatened by such activities.

Special projects personnel at One Call Concept's (OCC) Wichita, Kansas, Systems Division have created a pure object-oriented reusable development environment called "Mapping Software Libraries." Mapping Software Libraries (MSL) consists of libraries of reusable components which are used to create electronic mapping and geographical information systems applications. MSL is designed to be used for development of in-house applications, marketable applications, and as a stand alone product.

STATEMENT OF THE PROBLEM

For older versions of their mapping software, OCC used a third-party package for all mapping and Geographic Information Systems functionality. The disadvantages of this were threefold:

1. The functional breakdown and interface of the third-party package was not conducive to easily maintained, rapidly developed applications.

2. OCC was not allowed access to the source code for the package. This prevented them from making changes, enhancements or fixing minor bugs. Support and documentation by this third party was not sufficient for OCC's needs. Furthermore, certain applications had to be curtailed because of the lack of desired functionality.

3. The dependence on a third party for a critical component of their system left OCC vulnerable. If relations had soured or the third party had gone out of business, this would have left OCC in a serious bind.

153

SOLUTION: THE MAPPING SOFTWARE LIBRARY

For those reasons, OCC decided to proceed with their own library. Because they were developing their own software from scratch, the special projects team decided to lobby the management for permission to proceed with object-oriented technology. They were determined to show that object-oriented design and programming, along with a similar structured approach to the development process, could significantly reduce the time and cost of software development.

They developed a reliable working library in seven months, faster than any other in-house project of similar scope. Not only was the development faster, but the end product had fewer bugs, was easier to maintain, and performed better than the previous similar conventionally developed software products.

For example, their previous polygon library, developed in C under SCO Unix, had taken four person-weeks to test and debug. Their current Geometric library, which includes not only polygons but various other related classes such as LineSeg, Grid, etc., was developed in C++ using strict object-oriented methods. This library took about eight person-weeks to code, test, and debug. It is far more efficient, reliable and is much easier to use and maintain. They attribute this disparity to the benefits of a structured development approach in conjunction with object-oriented methods.

MSL consists of six libraries:

1. Abstract Data Type Library
ArgumentList, DoubleList, Error, MemoryManager, Option, Range, Set, SingleList, String, SystemParameter, Timer

2. Geometric Library
Grid, GridStore, Line, Point, Polygon, RotateableScaleableFont, Rectangular-Hull, Segment, Zone.

3. Graphical User Interface Library
Bell, Button, CheckBox, CommandMenu, CompletionField, Color, Cursor, CustomDialog, DataMenu, DistanceField, DrawWindow, ErrorDialog, Event, FileDialog, Form, GraphicalEnvironment, GraphicalInfo, InfoDialog, Labelled-TextField, Label, MainWindow, MenuBar, MessageDialog, Panel, PixelMap, PlaceSelector, PositionField, PromptDialog, QuestionDialog, Scale, ScrolledDraw-Window, ScrolledList, ScrolledTextWindow, TextField, TimerField, Warning-Dialog, WorkingDialog.

4. Geographical Database Library
Address, AsciiRec, BlockSet, CountyNameFile, DataFile, Feature, DataBase-Index, LogicalBlock, NameFile, Query, Overlay, OverlayManager, PlaceNameFile, StateNameFile, StringTable, TigerNameFile, TigerFeature, Trie.

5. Communications Library
Application, BackgroundTask, IdleProcedure.

6. Map Library
Map

The lowest level library, under which every other library is built is the ADT library. So in building the GUI library, much of the ADT library is used. The other libraries can be used independently, but not without the ADT library.

According to Dan Bernstein:

> On top of the ADT library is the geometric library. For example, take the line. A polygon is a list of points, so we need to use the list data type from the ADT to build it. The polygon library contains things like grid . . . RectangularHull. (Take any collection of points, a rectangular Hull would be the smallest rectangle containing all of those points.) We do our mapping on a county by county basis each containing map features like rivers, RR's, etc. so to know what the general area of our county is, we generate a rectangular hull to include all the features in the county. When the window, which is another rectangle, moves into that rectangular hull, we know to bring in that particular county.

The classes in each of the Libraries are designed to be used and reused independently, except where obvious dependencies occur. This allows each class to be reused and assembled with other classes, which is key to the business strategy of the company. This provides for rapidly deployed software for several key systems, geographic and otherwise, as well as custom applications for clients.

MSL was written in C++ and runs in Unix. In the future it will also be ported to other platforms such as MS Windows, OS/2, and OSF/1. All the machine and platform dependencies have been isolated to ease such a port.

The Libraries support a large number of users at any given time. Typical staffing at company managed call centers ranges from 1 to 75 users. By its nature, the business requires very fast screen refresh and data retrieval times. The number of users also requires more memory management than a typical application can perform. For this reason the Libraries have been designed to be fast and small.

One of the most important features of MSL is the ability to create and manipulate "smooth-scrolling" maps. The map window is backed up on the server side by a pixelmap of user specified proportions. The data need be drawn to the pixelmap once, eliminating the need for database queries for every scrolling operation. The database queries are performed only when the window crosses a pixelmap boundary.

MSL is independent from source data. Currently, applications are designed to be used with U.S. Census data. However, since MSL is source data independent, other conversion programs for other kinds of data may be easily written for use with the Library.

Exhibit 15.1   System components.

	Hardware	Software
Interface	HDS View Station (x terminals)	X Windows 11 R4 Motif 1.1
Core Code	Independent	GNU g++ C++ Compiler
Database	Independent	Proprietary
Development Environment	Wyse 9000i	GNU Emacs GNU gdb (debugger) GNU gmake GNU utilities

The graphical user interface Library provides special classes for use with geographic applications, but applications written using MSL need not be geographic. The user interface has been carefully designed for plug-in use with Motif-style, third party interface packages and provides more than enough support for other completely different applications.

Exhibit 15.1 lists MSL's major components. MSL contains approximately 66,000 lines of code, and uses the following object-oriented features:

BASIC OO FUNCTIONALITY
- Classes/Instances.
- Inheritance/specialization.
- Methods/messages.
- Virtual methods/polymorphism.

ADVANCED OO FUNCTIONALITY
- Dynamic class and method generation.

DEVELOPMENT ENVIRONMENT
- Automatic method tracing.
- Automatic links to databases.
- Editors, indexers, consistency checkers.

STORAGE MANAGEMENT
- Repository available.
- Version control.

CODE GENERATED
- Compiled code.

Exhibit 15.2 shows MSL's MainWindow object, which contains a MenuBar object, a ScrolledDrawWindow object, and a Panel object. In the upper left corner there are two cascading CommandMenu objects containing TextButton objects hanging from the MenuBar object. The Lowest Level CommandMenu demonstrates different colored text in the same object. The Panel object is on the extreme right and contains various multi-colored PictureButton objects. The rest of the screen is taken up by the ScrolledDrawWindow object, which is displaying a map, and contains a number of Symbol objects (the crosses and airplanes). The map has been copied from a pixelmap object four times the size of the window, and can be scrolled smoothly by using the ScrollBar objects.

The lower screen shows the pop-up IdentifyDialog window.

Exhibit 15.3 (1-7) shows the MSL Object Hierarchy.

PROJECT LIFE CYCLE

MSL was developed in-house by Daniel J. Bernstein, Manager of Special Projects and Mohammad Jafar. They were assisted by outside consultants, Robert Reed, Robert Zembowicz, Scott Dysinger, and Dianne Ngyuen.

The 66,000 lines of code were completed in a period of fifteen months using four full time staff.

Analysis and Design

MSL was One Call Concept's first endeavor in object-oriented programming. Because of this Daniel Bernstein, Manager of Special Projects, had to sell top management on the OO approach. Bernstein drafted the first requirements document. He and Mohammad Jafar designed the object classes, using class diagrams like those in Exhibit 15.3.

Selling the object-oriented approach was not easy, because no one in the company including the people on the project had any experience in this matter. But, a more conventional procedural approach was ruled out early, because the problem so obviously lent itself to object-oriented analysis.

Bernstein explains the appeal of OO at this stage:

> Just take the map for example. Everything about a map is basically a representation of the physical world. One of the great things about OO development is that the objects in the program correspond to objects in the real world as much as possible. There's always some grey areas about how to represent the analog in a digital environment. But you have this entity called a map which is a representation of the world, and you have this thing called an object which is also, ideally, a representation of the world. So the two fit very well. You can take a map and make it an object and say what about the map, what real world objects are being

Exhibit 15.2   Main window object.

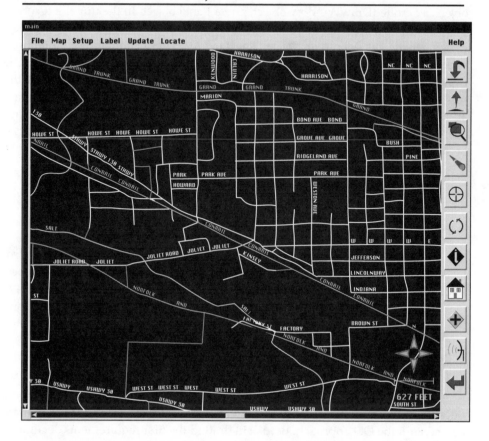

represented by this map? Ok a map has a rotation, it has a scale, etc. And you can break it into sub-components, such as railroads, a railroad is an object, and a road is an object and a river is an object. And you can take all the commonalities between all railroads or all rivers, and combine them into what we call a feature. And the features can get more specific. And it's all very straightforward to say to look at the system as how to represent it as a real world thing instead of asking what does a river do or what does a road do, which is how you'd approach it if you were using a functional approach.

We look at things and we say, let's make this an object first and then discuss what methods we can associate with it. Once we have the objects we ask, what is this object responsible for, for instance scale is responsible for telling the user miles per inch. So the scale has to take care of that. The map doesn't have to know about scale. The compass takes care of the rotation.

Exhibit 15.2 Continued

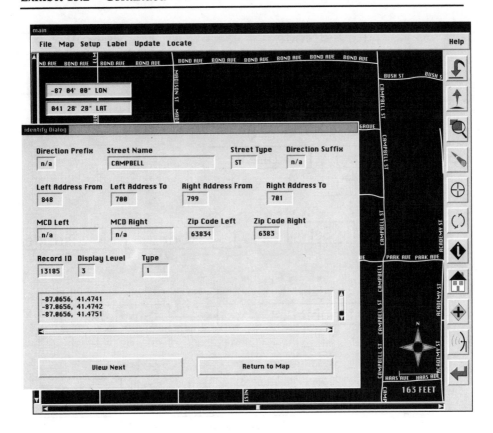

Development

For each class, the low-level design outlined a set of test suites before the code could be released. There were code reviews for quality assurance and the class was not released until it was thoroughly tested. This had the effect of minimizing bugs.

The development team was divided as follows:

Designers/Coders: Daniel Bernstein, Robert Zembowicz, and Mohammad Jafar

Coders/Designers: Scott Dysinger

Coders: Robert Reed, Dianne Ngyuen

Exhibit 15.3.1 through 15.3.7   MSL class diagrams.

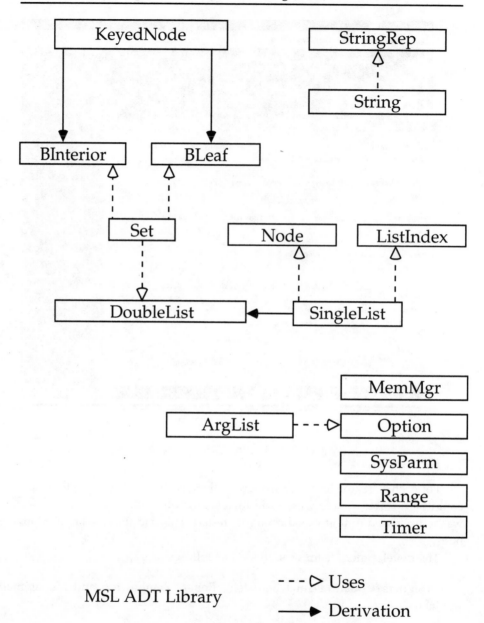

MSL ADT Library

Exhibit 15.3.2   MSL class diagrams.

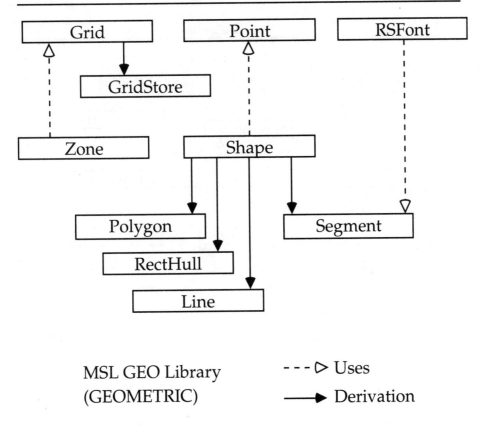

MSL GEO Library
(GEOMETRIC)

- - - ▷ Uses

⟶ Derivation

Seven C++ compilers were tried on the WYSE Unix, none of which were fully functional. For a while development was seriously hampered until GCC 2.1 was released. From that point on they used GNU products, which worked nicely with GNU Emacs.

Deployment

MSL is currently in Beta test.

Maintenance

The same personnel will be maintaining MSL. Maintenance is expected to be very minimal. The library is interdependent enough that most bugs were discov-

Exhibit 15.3.3   MSL class diagrams.

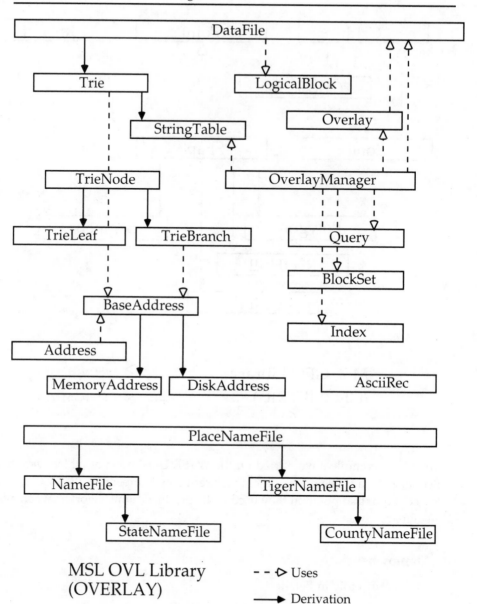

MSL OVL Library
(OVERLAY)

- - ▷ Uses

⟶ Derivation

Exhibit 15.3.4 MSL class diagrams.

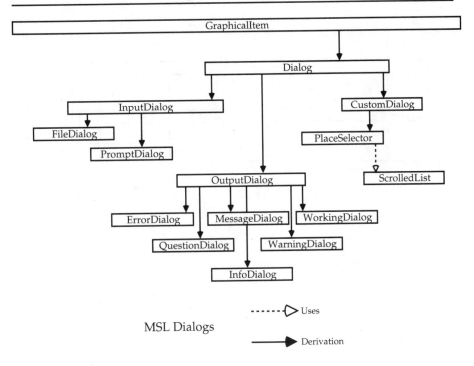

MSL Dialogs

Exhibit 15.3.5 MSL class diagrams.

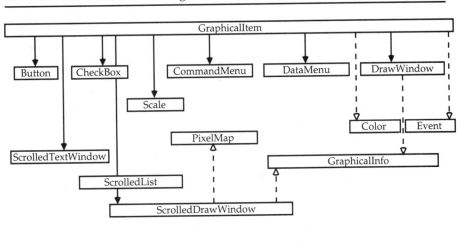

MSL GUI Library (1)

Exhibit 15.3.6   MSL class diagrams.

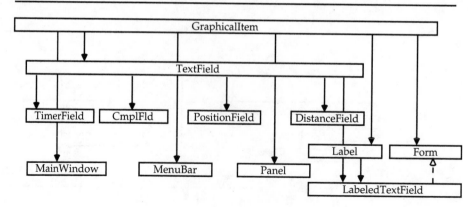

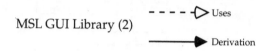

MSL GUI Library (2)   - - - - ▷ Uses

                         ─────▶ Derivation

Exhibit 15.3.7   MSL class diagrams.

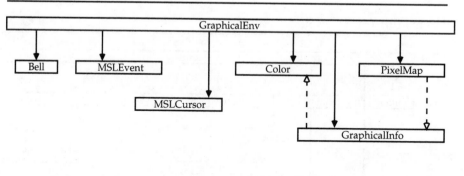

MSL GUI Library (3)   - - - - ▷ Uses

                         ─────▶ Derivation

ered early. According to Mohammad Jafar, OO is of great benefit in maintaining a system. "Because control is more localized in classes, bugs are easier to catch." Other benefits he cited were reusability, flexibility, and the generic nature of some classes.

BENEFITS

According to Bernstein, OCC is quite happy with the results of the MSL project.

> We no longer have to depend on the limitations of a third party library. At the same time our final products are more flexible and can be improved further by improving our library. The flexibility of the library and the reusability of a big portion of the code is attributed mostly to the object-oriented approach.

The OO approach reduced the development time compared to previous projects developed in C by at least half. Maintenance expense is expected to be reduced because of fewer bugs.

OO will enable One Call Concepts to develop more flexible and efficient applications using one-fifth the size of previous similar applications. OO will help OCC to respond to new demands because the data encapsulations of OO enable easy modifications to some classes without affecting any other classes that use it, because the public interface never changes.

OCC's ability to develop new types of applications is greatly enhanced because the entire library code is reusable. OCC already has five applications planned and waiting for the final release of MSL.

CONCLUSIONS

The project team learned much from this development effort:

1. We gained considerable experience in object-oriented design and programming.
2. By using an object-oriented approach we realized that there are many ways in which speed can be attained. For example, in a conventional approach, a developer may never think of keeping the length of a string. Instead, the developer would recompute the string every time it is needed. The recomputation approach may have been a great idea in the past when memory was scarce and expensive, but it is no longer a primary concern. Now, by introducing a String class that keeps the string length as a data member, getting the string length becomes a $0(1)$ operation, independent of the length of the string. This example may not apply to all procedural languages, however, it does apply to C. The time spent in recom-

putations can be overwhelming when strings are used in recursive structures. Although this point is rarely mentioned in object-oriented literature, it is a very important one to address. As a software engineer, one has to remember that most algorithms were developed at a time when memory concerns were of great importance.

3. Object-oriented design clarifies the overall system design by localizing different design issues to the various classes. Module separation and inter-modular dependencies become clearer due to encapsulation and information hiding. The changes applied to one module do not affect other modules as long as the interface is not changed.

4. After we had developed an ADT library, we discovered many excellent public-domain libraries that were superior to our own ADT package. We think we did a lot of unnecessary work, especially in the ADT package. We have learned a valuable lesson concerning reuse.

The MSL project forced OCC to formulate in-house designing and coding standards. They had to invent an entire set of standards for project-member communication and overall organization. Due to the success of the project, OCC's Systems Division is considering the object-oriented approach as the company standard for problem solving.

For others considering similar efforts, Jafar advises,

> Spend sufficient time investigating existing libraries. We think we lost on the issue of reuse, mainly because we did not spend enough time analyzing existing libraries. Two good examples of public-domain libraries for C++ are NIHCL and COOL. Both libraries come with source code and a users manual. These libraries could also serve a team as good models of the object-oriented approach.

CHAPTER 16

Application Description

BUSINESS AND MANAGEMENT SUPPORT SYSTEM

The Civil Aviation Authority is a statutory authority controlled by government. As such it acts as a regulatory body while promoting the public service aspect of UK civil aviation. Its functions include operation of the air traffic system, monitoring air safety in all its facets, dealing with the economic regulation of civil aviation—particularly with respect to the air traveller—and advising the UK government on aeronautical matters.

STATEMENT OF THE PROBLEM

CAA managers spend much of their time looking for, analyzing, and presenting information. Information is not easily accessible and often requires tremendous people resources in order to collect, interpret, and format it for presentation. The dynamic nature of the airline industry, coupled with rapidly changing regulatory requirements, requires a system's environment that is easy to use, rapid to implement, and quick to change.

A large amount of information is presented to managers in hardcopy format. Though computers are available in notebook configurations, making them extremely portable, in many situations it is either not viable or appropriate to take them into meetings and presentations in order to have information instantly available. Battery life is limited and the presence of a computer in formal business settings can be awkward. Furthermore, senior executives are comfortable with paper-based output. It is portable and easy to reproduce. As a result, hardcopy needs to be produced as a companion format.

With the advent of desktop publishing, spread sheets, laser printers, etc., users expect publication quality output. This output includes the integration of text, graphics, and images. Report writing software produces traditional "green bar" formats of rows and columns. Often decision makers are only interested in a few numbers. In order to achieve publication quality presentations it requires that the user works with many products and manipulates by hand the information into a quality format. What is required are systems that provide output which leverages publication quality standards. Further, outputs need to accommodate different notebook sizes (e.g., A4, A5, etc.) so that reports can be incorporated into time management diary formats: the primary information tool that people carry with them.

Information within the CAA is machine readable and non-machine readable (e.g., documents, letters, scraps of paper, index cards). Machine readable information is in support of the operational elements of the enterprise such as personnel, financial, sector information. Operational data is micro-focussed and encompasses vast quantities of data which is virtually useless in support of strategic decisions due to their detailed focus. However, if processed and electronically analyzed, this data can form the foundation for providing the "32,000 foot macro view" of the organization.

There are many other pieces of information which are equally important, but which are not readily available in machine readable format. These sources include information which has been written on calendars, in diaries, on index cards, or on document printouts. Typical non-machine-readable information concerns project status, project managers, vendor contacts, contract values, anticipated projects, ideas, suggestions, and observations. Some sources of information may be shared while others are confidential or even personal. What is needed for effective decision making is to have a Business and Management Support System which provides a seamless integration of operational, group, personal information management and publication quality hardcopy.

SOLUTION: BUSINESS AND MANAGEMENT SUPPORT SYSTEM

CAA's Business and Management Support System addresses personal and organizational information requirements of senior managers and executives. The system allows individuals to access both local and shared databases. Given that end-users are busy, interfaces to BMSS must be obvious and usable without training or documentation.

BMSS is divided into four segments. The first segment is personal office management. This facet includes:

- Rolodex (encompassing managing information by business, supplier, leisure, travel, personal, miscellaneous, and employees) which automatically publishes directories;

- Time Management (day-at-a-glance, week-at-a-glance, month-at-a-glance) which publishes A5 formatted publication quality diaries;

- List Management which manages lists of information by category and sub-organized by date; and

- Note Management, similar to list management.

The second segment focuses on presenting numeric information about financial views, air traffic control sector information, projects, head count, etc. Numerical information is managed through interfaces which deliver numeric capture, manipulation, data management, and graphical/report format. An equivalent to spreadsheets, without the crypticism associated with spreadsheet technology, and providing more flexibility.

The third element is focused on Project Management. Currently project management entails Pert, Bant, and CPM representations of plans. Little software support is available which tracks and manages a project once it is underway. Current project management facilities concentrate on developing plans outlining the step-by-step implementation of the goal. BMSS includes the ability to capture information regarding project status, manage, related vendors, budget, actual, and milestones. BMSS compares a project's current status with the plan.

The fourth element is Human Resource Management. Large enterprises such as the CAA require the creation and management of organizational structures which group together personnel as well as cross relationships. The development of organization structures is laborious, utilizing desktop publishing or other drawing routines. The key is that these structures, which identify where an individual belongs and associated organizational goals, are lost in constantly updated, manually generated organization charts. BMSS provides the facility to navigate through organizational structures on screen and retrieve associated information such as Priority Based budgeting parameters, goals, objectives, projects, and budgets.

The user interface of BMSS consists of a combination of the fourteen class objects available within MacroScope. The MacroScope class objects are window, button, composite, menu, text_box, scanner, message_box, package_manager, pie_chart, variance_graph, bar_graph, line_graph, stacker_graph, and organization_chart.

The window is the parent object. Windows have a parent/child relationship with objects based on their display_list definition. By manipulating the display_list of a window, windows may be re-formatted or other objects re-used to create new screens. The use of states within buttons, composites, text_boxes, and package_managers, allows developers to attach multiple functionality lists to one object definition.

Entire processes are reusable within an application and between applications. The package_manager class object supports the passing of variables. The variables are swapped with the contents of a clipboard, a text_box, or a hard-coded string during runtime. The use of package_managers greatly reduces the amount of in-line code required to process a function.

Exhibit 16.1   BMSS desktop.

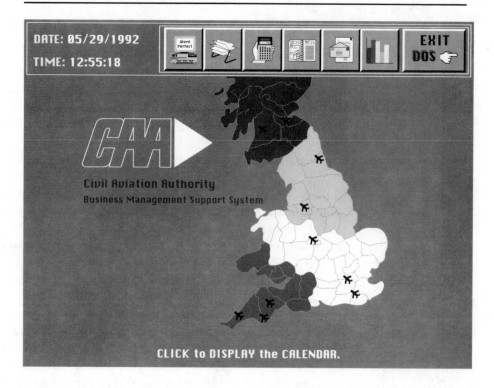

Exhibit 16.1 shows the BMSS desktop. Images are used to provide visual sizzle.

Exhibit 16.2 illustrates an organizational chart. The levels of the organizational chart are viewed by either title or name. The TRAVERSE button allows the user to move between levels. The organizational chart supports a drill down facility which enables the user to access personnel details on an individual.

The screen in Exhibit 16.3 shows a line graph. A message__box is part of the line__graph and when the user moves the mouse over a point on the line__graph, a numeric equivalent value displays in the message__box.

All elements of BMSS publish A4 or A5 reports including integrated graphics where applicable. Format and size are dependent on modules and their associated requirements. BMSS uses highly graphical user interfaces coupled with dynamic help, that can be used without training and documentation. Dynamic Help is a powerful help facility that broadcasts instantly what will happen if the mouse is clicked, whenever the mouse is over an object which can be invoked. Additional capabilities which aid the user are viewer windows associated with graphs. For

Exhibit 16.2   Organizational chart.

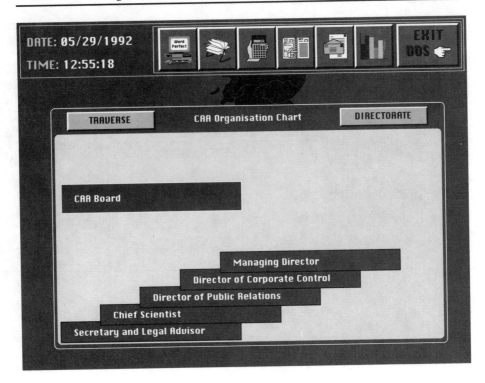

example, stacking bar graphs have three view windows which broadcast values immediately whenever the mouse is positioned over a business graphics component such as a bar or wedge or point. One window reflects the raw value of the rectangle, the second shows the rectangle's percentage of the whole, and the third reflects the total of all the stacked bars.

BASIC OO FUNCTIONALITY
  – Classes/instances.
  – Inheritance/specialization.
  – Methods/messages.
  – Virtual methods/polymorphism.

ADVANCED OO FUNCTIONALITY
  – Persistent objects.
  – Dynamic class/method generation.
  – Constraint programming.

Exhibit 16.3   Line graph.

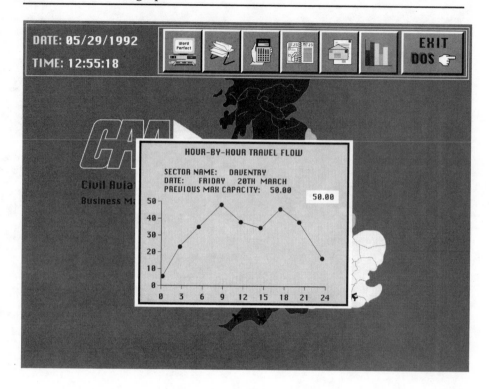

EXTENDED PROGRAMMING ENVIRONMENT
- Functional programming.
- Inference/rule-based programming.

DEVELOPMENT ENVIRONMENT
- Graphical developer interface.
- Interpreted internal language
- Graphical browsers.
- Automatic method tracing.
- Automatic links to databases.
- Internal/external class libraries.
- Class libraries interpreted.
- Editors, indexers, consistency checkers.
- Graphical tool for user interface development.
- Tools for target operating system interface layout available.

Exhibit 16.4   System components.

	Hardware	Software
Interface	PC Client, SUN Server, Ethernet LAN	MacroScope
Core Code	PC Client, SUN Server, Ethernet LAN	MacroScope
Database	PC Client, SUN Server, Ethernet LAN	MacroScope (client and server), and Sybase server
Development Environment	PC Client, SUN Server, Ethernet LAN	MacroScope "5GL" development environment

STORAGE MANAGEMENT
   – Repository available.
   – Version control available.

CODE GENERATION
   – Language code generated.
   – Compiled code generated.

PROJECT LIFE CYCLE

Like the other MacroScope applications described in this book, development of BMSS was nearly instantaneous. Elapsed time, including analysis, design, and development was about two months, requiring a little over 1000 person-hours.

BENEFITS

Please see the chapter on United Artists' Concessions Management (ECIS) for a discussion of MacroScope.

Domain: Administration

Business administration has become increasingly complex in recent years as companies become more varied and change more rapidly over time. This complexity leads to some difficult challenges in developing and maintaining software to support administrative operations.

Consider the relatively mundane task of managing employee benefits. There was once a time when this task was tedious but manageable. Everyone received pretty much the same package of benefits, and it was relatively easy to construct software to track those benefits. Today, "cafeteria-style" benefits are all the rage, and the mix of benefits varies not only from one company to the next but from one person to the next within any given company.

That variation presented a major problem for Hewitt Associates, which helps companies manage their benefits and compensation programs. The complexity of the mix-and-match combinations clearly calls for electronic support, but that same complexity makes developing general-purpose software very difficult. The problem is that a general program would require so much customization to meet the needs of any one client that it would become a piece of hand-crafted software, complete with its own maintenance requirements.

Hewitt's solution was to use object technology to construct a set of benefit modules that can be combined in any mixture to meet a company's needs. The encapsulation of objects was used to ensure that these modules would work together in any combination. With this system, Hewitt can ship the collection of modules that precisely meets each client's needs. The problem of maintenance is minimized, however, because the component modules can all be maintained independently. If any one module changes, all the clients that are using that module can be updated quickly and efficiently.

Thomas Cook, a British travel agency serving multinational businesses, is faced with the problem of administering travel activities spanning many different countries, languages, time zones, and currencies. In response to the increasing information load, the company used object technology to develop a global information system. Within five months, they built a system that provided a uniform graphical interface and completely insulated users from the international differences.

Westinghouse Savannah River Company was faced with a different problem of administration: the mass of paperwork had become so great within their organization that it was difficult for people to keep track of what they were supposed to read and what they were supposed to do about it. To help ease this problem, the company built a system called Linkup to extract structure and relationships from textual data and present it in simple graphical form. For example, Linkup has been used to integrate several mainframe databases and provide a graphical overview of the organization. Users can browse through the org chart, identifying the functions of the 2,000 organizations and 19,000 people who make up the organization. The system has also been used to place all policies on line so that users can follow hypertext trails to the answers they need.

To date, the company has measured significant increases in productivity due to the immediate access to critical information. Employees can now get answers about who is doing what and how their actions are affected by policies quickly and easily. The result is better-informed employees, more clearly defined roles, and better access to policies. There has also been a significant reduction in cost due to the elimination of paper documents.

Each of the three applications in this section illustrates the benefits of object-oriented technology for rapid software development. More importantly, they illustrate how genuine business benefits can be obtained with the technology. This illustrates once again our contention that we are beginning to see a second wave of benefits that goes beyond software productivity to increase organizational productivity. This is, after all, the whole point of building management information systems.

CHAPTER 17

Application Description

TOTAL BENEFIT ADMINISTRATION™

STATEMENT OF THE PROBLEM

Hewitt Associates is an international management consulting firm specializing in the design, financing, administration and communication of employee benefits and compensation programs. Their services are used by large organizations in a variety of business sectors. Hewitt has 3000 associates located in 61 offices around the world.

One of the fastest growing, and most complex, areas of their practice is helping organizations administer employee benefit plans, especially 401(k) and other defined contribution plans, flexible benefit plans, and defined benefit pension plans. The administrative burden on employers is more cumbersome today than in the past.

Among large organizations, there is almost universal offering of 401(k), or "self-directed" retirement plans. Among other things, these plans require tracing of employee monies deferred into the plan (pre-tax and after-tax), monitoring of individual deferral amounts (to comply with government rules), recordkeeping on the investment options elected, and processing of certain special events, for instance loans and withdrawals.

Among medium and large employers, flexible benefit, so-called "cafeteria," plans are fast becoming the norm. These plans require not only tracking of individual employee elections in each benefit area, but also recordkeeping on information that is quite different than that retained for 401(k) purposes. For example, choices in medical coverage are frequently offered. As a result, the employer is required to know not only which plan the employee selected, but also a variety of other information such as age/gender/number of dependents, primary care physician for each person covered under managed care options, or health habits if the plan provides credits for certain life-style related factors.

In the pension area, administration is inherently complex, compounded by a growing body of legislation and regulation intended to make plans more responsive to public policy concerns.

The problem faced by Hewitt Associates was to build a large-scale administrative system. Such a solution would have to meet five requirements:

1. The system must be tailored to meet the individual needs of diverse clients. At a summary level it appears that all clients follow a consistent approach to administration, but in practice each client has its own administrative nuances. For each client assignment, Hewitt didn't want to build from scratch, instead they wanted to have a strong base set of functionality that could be easily re-used and extended to build tailored systems.

2. The system must have a low maintenance obligation. From a base software development perspective, Hewitt is encountering more demanding client requirements. Also there is the ongoing need to incorporate legislative and regulatory requirements as they are promulgated. As the number of Hewitt's clients grows so does the ongoing maintenance obligation. Hewitt needed to be able to deliver updates to current clients in a cost-effective and timely manner.

3. The system must provide multiple front-end access to common business functions. There is a growing set of users of the system each requiring their own interface and access to information. For example, plan participants want timely access to their account balances and the ability to process transactions against their accounts; plan administrators need access to inform the participants of their retirement options; plan recordkeepers need to process large volumes of accounting transactions. To meet these needs, the systems needed a variety of user interfaces, including GUI, Voice Response Interface for employees and a Telephone Support Center staffed with knowledgeable account representatives. To reduce development costs and help ease maintenance issues, Hewitt required that these interfaces access and execute a common set of business function logic.

4. The system must allow upgrades for new technologies. Hewitt wanted to be able to take advantage of new or emerging technologies and architectures. They wanted to move from a VSAM data management environment to a relational database mode. They wanted to implement a client-server or cooperative processing architecture to better distribute the application code to the right platforms while still maintaining flexibility, and to deliver the system on multiple server platforms. They also wanted to use new presentation hardware, such as graphic and multi-media workstation and voice response equipment.

5. The system must provide one integrated software solution across business functions. For those clients selecting multiple administrative services for different types of benefit plans, Hewitt wanted to ensure that the system looked and felt like one integrated system. This required a common graphical interface, common approaches to processing employee events/transactions, and common approaches to interfacing with external systems.

SOLUTION: TOTAL BENEFIT ADMINISTRATION™ SYSTEM

TBA was designed using object technology from the ground up, from analysis through implementation. What makes the TBA approach interesting is that it deploys object technology using traditional tools such as COBOL, CICS, DB2, and APPC. TBA's cooperative processing architecture provides for multiple front-end clients accessing a back-end server. The back-end server contains the core business logic and relational database access. The initial implementation of the server was on an IBM mainframe. The server architecture is designed to run across a range of machines from PC to mainframe.

Exhibit 17.1 lists TBA's major components. TBA's client-server architecture consists of two object-oriented components, respectively located on the mainframe server and the client PCs. The mainframe component consists of a series of classes, implemented with Hewitt's own object-oriented COBOL extensions, representing all activities and components available on the server. These mainframe classes

Exhibit 17.1   System components.

	Hardware	Software
Interface	IBM PC comp	Choreographer, "C", OS2 Comm Mgr., CICS, Remote Procedure Call Software
Core Code	IBM Server	COBOL, COBOL OOP Preprocessor
Database	IBM Server	DB/2, OS/2 Data Manager or any SQL compatible RDB
Development Environment	IBM PC, Token Ring LAN	OS/2 LAN Manager, OS/2 Data Manager, Micro Focus COBOL, Choreographer

provide the core business functionality and processing models (e.g., Person, PensionPlan, UserProfile, PersonActivity), and encapsulate the relational database access for persistent storage and query access. Activity is an abstract class representing activities which the user can initiate. Activity is implemented as a list of Function instances that make up the Activity. Function instances are made up of Panels, abstract user interface descriptions, and Transactions, and actual database interactions.

The PC component, implemented using the Choreographer application development environment, interprets Panels sent from the mainframe to present the user with a highly interactive user interface. Each Activity object on the mainframe creates a WorkList on the PC. Each item on the WorkList corresponds to a Function in the Activity, and a panel to input event data. The WorkList manages a series of forms, corresponding to the mainframe Panel Objects. TBA can also execute certain mainframe Activity objects using voice response over the telephone.

In the mainframe server implementation, the two components are connected through IBM SNA APPC (LU 6.2) network session services. On the PC end, an internally developed Remote Procedure Call (RPC) program provides the PC with an API interface to the mainframe server. All PC communication session management and data conversion services are provided by the RPC software. In addition to the communication services, CICS provides the connection to the COBOL objects implementing core business services and the DB2 database system.

TBA employs objects at every level. Each user activity is represented by a mainframe object that encapsulates all relevant user interface, validation, error management, and database access for that transaction. Inheritance and polymorphism are exploited to reuse shared aspects of these transactions. All server classes are developed in COBOL using Hewitt's internally developed object COBOL syntax. This source code is run through their own COBOL Object Oriented Language (COOL) preprocessor to create the actual platform target code, either batch, CICS, or PC. The code is then compiled and placed in the target environment for execution.

Mainframe objects create PC objects to describe a graphic user interface that is actually created and managed on the PC. These user interface descriptions are implemented with objects on the PC that represent, for example, GUI buttons, data entry fields, help text, etc. Polymorphism between the PC user interface components allows for much simplified implementation of the components that execute the objects passed from the mainframe. The user interface provides object-oriented forms and a framework that allow a user to easily navigate from form to form, organize related forms, and organize related tasks for a particular user. Finally, in another example of polymorphism, the voice response component can share some of the same mainframe objects that can be used from the GUI, but through telephone voice response.

Exhibit 17.2 shows two screens demonstrating the TBA forms management metaphor. On top, the user is working with John Q. Sample and doing the

Exhibit 17.2   Forms management screens.

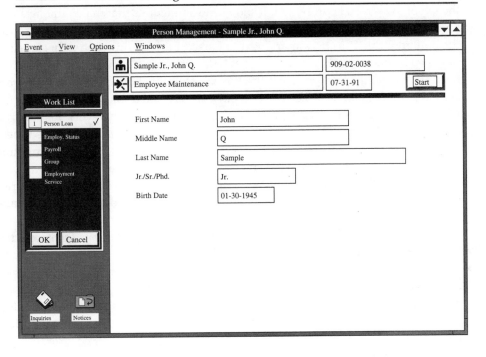

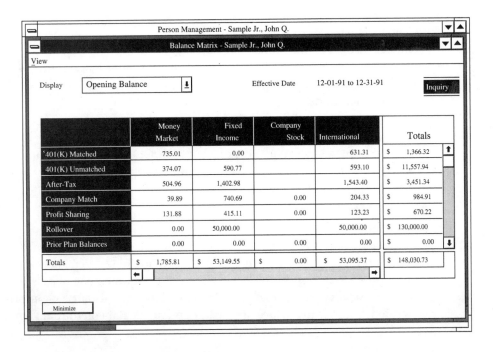

Employee Maintenance activity. Once this activity was selected, the Work List on the left of the screen is presented. It shows the 5 functions that make up Employee Maintenance. The Person Basic function is highlighted and presents its form on the bottom right. The check mark next to Person Basic indicates that this function has been accessed. Users navigate through the other functions and their associated forms by selecting functions from the Work List. In the bottom screen, a different activity, Home Loan, is selected. Here the user has asked for help about a particular field in the form. User actions such as moving from one Work List item to another, or selecting OK at the bottom of the Work List, initiate events where messages are sent to server objects. Ultimately, these messages return information for display on the PC and make changes to the server database.

Exhibit 17.3 shows informational views available from TBA. On top, the Person Inquiry activity has been selected, showing a series of reports and worksheets that can be examined. Each of these can be examined in detail by clicking on the icon, as shown on the bottom. Each report is created by server object that executes and returns information to the PC for display.

The class design of the system is proprietary information. There are approximately 1500 classes with 6000 methods defined on the back-end server, and 500 classes defined for the GUI. Approximately half of these classes are used to define method protocol structures. In general, the classes are component parts of Employees, Benefits Plans, and Administrative Activities.

TBA employs the following OO features:

BASIC OO FUNCTIONALITY
- Classes/Instances.
- Inheritance/specialization.
  The OO-COBOL environment supports single inheritance, which was sufficient to implementing the server methods. The Choreographer environment supports multiple inheritance.
- Methods/messages.
- Virtual methods/polymorphism.
  Hewitt implemented polymorphism in their OO-COBOL environment. Choreographer is an un-typed language and supports a non inheritance-based polymorphism.

ADVANCED OO FUNCTIONALITY
- Persistent objects.
  IBM's DB2 relational database is used to store data on the server. Since DB2 is not object-oriented and does not provide object persistence, the application was responsible for translating the in-memory objects into the relational database. Each class that contained persistent data implemented methods to retrieve, insert and update the data on the data base.

Exhibit 17.3   Person inquiry screen.

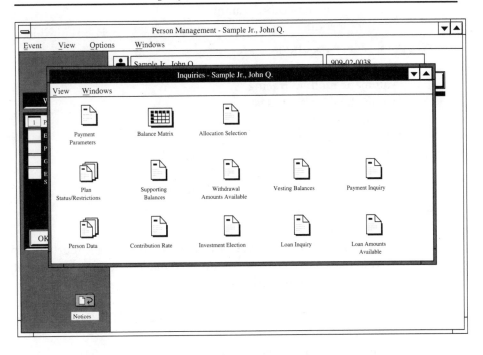

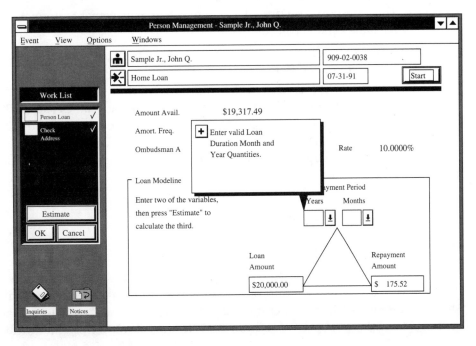

EXTENDED PROGRAMMING ENVIRONMENT
– Inference/rule-based programming.

The Aion product was used to build the client setup subsystem.

DEVELOPMENT ENVIRONMENT
– Graphical developer interface.
– Automatic method tracing.
– Automatic links to databases.
– Internal/external class libraries.
– Class libraries interpreted.
– Editors, indexers, consistency checkers.
– Graphical tool for user interface development.
– Tools for target operating system interface layout available.

STORAGE MANAGEMENT
– Repository available.

An extensive repository was developed to store the important project information such as class, method, and data base definition information. The information was used to generate control tables for the OO-COBOL pre-compiler, DB2 SQL, and to generate the method's external protocols and internal data structures (copybooks) for both the COBOL and Choreographer code.

– Version control available.

The repository also provides configuration management information to facilitate version control.

CODE GENERATION
– Language code generated.

The system uses an OO-COBOL pre-compiler to produce standard ANSI COBOL. The programmers write their source code in an Object COBOL language syntax. This pre-COBOL code is processed through the COOL pre-processor to create the COBOL code that is then compiled into object code for the target environment. The repository also generates the copybooks that are used for internal data structures and method protocols.

PROJECT LIFE CYCLE

Analysis and Design

Because TBA was at the heart of Hewitt's business, the analysis and design phase was conducted by senior project leaders and senior management including the business practice leader and the Chief Information Officer. They followed their own methodology loosely based on the Wirfs-Brock object-oriented design approach (C-R-C method). They found that the absence of established method-ologies and support tools for large scale projects was a major drawback.

During this phase an internally developed repository was used to store vital class, method and protocol information. They also used the Bachman Analyst tool to develop an entity-relationship diagram for the physical database design. They used WordPerfect to write detailed logic specifications and Harvard Graphics for the class organization and relationship diagrams.

The project team included Sanjiv Anand, project manager, and Jerry Fahling, Tim Hilgenberg, Jim McGhee, Jane Nunes, and Scott Woldridge. They received assistance from GUIdance Technologies, Inc.

Development

To develop TBA, Hewitt followed a traditional large-scale construction approach. The team was split up into core business service development, VRS interface development, GUI (Choreographer) development, and report develop-ment.

Deployment

TBA is currently in Beta Test.

BENEFITS

According to Tim Hilgenberg, the overall benefit was that upon completion of the system development, they had a library of quality reusable components and business function models that can quickly be assembled into a tailored software solution for their clients. The end result of having these components is that they have a high-quality software solution that is flexible enough to meet the needs of a diverse client base, and adaptable enough to meet the changing needs of the business environment.

Hilgenberg also made the following observations:

> The overall development costs were higher for the initial object-oriented development than for a traditional structured development, but now that we have an established set of classes and a robust technical architecture, the cost of future development will be lower.
>
> Reduced maintenance expense was very important to us. With the number of systems we are going to deploy, we needed an approach that would ease our maintenance burden. Since we deal in an area that is governed by a large and a complex body of law and regulations, there is always a high probability of change. We strongly feel that the use of OO would position us to quickly respond to changes, both competitive and legislative in a short period of time.

CONCLUSIONS

Hilgenberg offers the following advice to others contemplating similar projects:

The training and education of the team in OO technology is critical to the success of any mission critical software development. We underestimated the amount of time and education required to make the paradigm shift from structured to OO methods. Experience and an understanding of the concepts are the keys to effective class design. Also, sufficient time and attention needs to be paid to training. The entire team, from managers to end-users, needs extensive training in OO techniques. Prototyping real-world problems is particularly useful in that it helps reinforce the developers' understanding of OO in an application context. Also, before jumping into a mission critical application, it is helpful to gain experience and reinforce the techniques through a small prototype project.

Although most experts say that the selection of tools and programming environment can be postponed until after the design effort, in reality, given the current maturity of object technical architecture, it is very important to identify or develop a robust technical platform. This is especially true in developing a cooperative or client-server application on an IBM mainframe or a LAN server. The selection of non-object oriented tools and integrating them into a technical platform can be tricky. The technical platform needs to include a variety of tools such as programming languages, a relational data base, a GUI development tool, communication software, and a transaction processor. These tools should be assembled and tested and a small prototype built before a mission critical software project begins.

If you are developing a large scale system, you need to have a repository to store important project related information. On large developments, many issues arise due to size and it is critical to have a repository. Easy access to critical information helps to promote the reuse of classes and methods and provides the development team with the capability to generate some code and copybook members. Also, a repository function helps promote consistent terminology and project standards.

Finally, before starting a major project, an OO development methodology needs to be created. This methodology will help guide the team through the various phases of the development cycle and assist in the overall project management. You can develop your own approach, but there is currently a large volume of literature on development approaches. These approaches are in a more mature state and can be applied successfully to large scale development projects.

CHAPTER 18

Application Description

THOMAS COOK GLOBAL MIS

STATEMENT OF THE PROBLEM

International business travel is undergoing major changes. In the UK alone, over 20 billion is spent by companies on travel and entertainment. This reflects growth in all markets and particularly in Europe where air traffic is expected to double by the end of the 1990s. With travel becoming a more significant element of company expenses, travel managers will require better support to manage their costs.

Thomas Cook specializes in business travel services to multi-national organizations, and its current strategy requires it to present in summarized format, worldwide company travel data and information to its clients. Thomas Cook has many systems around the world that hold this data, running on a variety of hardware and applications environments. The priority is to be able to offer key corporate client travel managers summarized information for all markets, using the available data, in a format that can be easily understood. Thomas Cook's Global MIS application was developed to address this major goal, delivering reports with high quality graphical and textual output.

SOLUTION: GLOBAL MIS

Thomas Cook's Global MIS was built with MacroScope. It's main function of validation, consolidation, and reporting on multi-sourced corporate client data from Thomas Cook Network Members throughout the world, was previously not possible.

Monthly reservation systems data sent to Thomas Cook's Worldwide Headquarters as flat files, in different formats, are validated, translated and consolidated into a central Sybase database by a group of loaders. These loaders use validation databases that can be manipulated through the Global MIS on-line application, as Look-up tables different for each Network Member, to check if

Exhibit 18.1   Client summary screen.

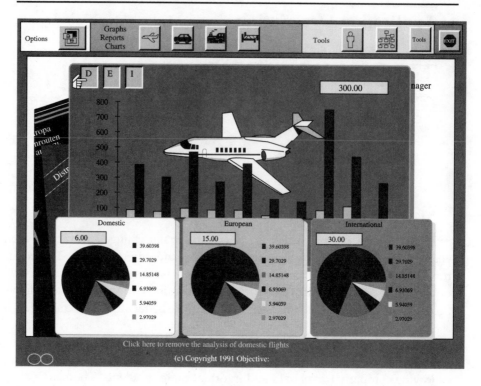

specific values are valid and if any translation is needed in order to consolidate the data. For example, "AA" may be the consolidated airline code for American Airlines, while "Amer" may be a valid code that needs to be translated to "AA" before it is loaded into the system.

When the monthly data have been loaded, the on-line application is then used to generate a number of reports, monthly and year-to-date, for corporate clients. Reports can be configured to include any combination of specific Network Member data.

Exhibit 18.1 shows GLOBAL MIS output screen with costs in ($ 000's) as a bar chart for yearly air travel, car hire, and hotel accommodation. Also a pie chart shows variance from previous years' prices. Exhibit 18.2 shows a company's airfare expenditures by airline, as a pie chart. Exhibit 18.3 lists Global MIS' major components. Global MIS was created by consultants from Objective International, Ltd., using MacroScope, an object-oriented "5GL," designed to access, and manipulate data from a variety of database systems and formats. Exhibit 18.4 shows the architecture of MacroScope.

Exhibit 18.2   Monthly air spending by airline.

WORLD INCORPORATED

CONSOLIDATED AIRLINE SPEND (US$) BY CLASS

JUNE 1992 - MONTHLY REPORT

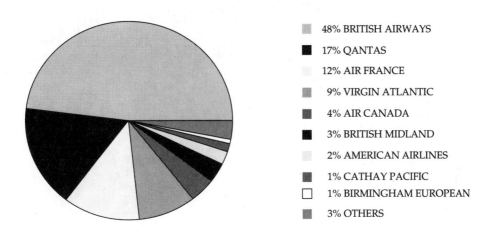

- 48% BRITISH AIRWAYS
- 17% QANTAS
- 12% AIR FRANCE
- 9% VIRGIN ATLANTIC
- 4% AIR CANADA
- 3% BRITISH MIDLAND
- 2% AMERICAN AIRLINES
- 1% CATHAY PACIFIC
- 1% BIRMINGHAM EUROPEAN
- 3% OTHERS

Exhibit 18.3   System components.

	Hardware	*Software*
Interface	PC Client, PS/2 Server Novell Token Ring	MacroScope
Core Code	PC Client, PS/2 Server Novell Token Ring	MacroScope
Database	PC Client, PS/2 Server Novell Token Ring	MacroScope (client and server)
Development Environment	PC Client, PS/2 Server Novell Token Ring	MacroScope "5GL" development environment

BASIC OO FUNCTIONALITY

– Classes/Instances.

MacroScope is comprised of large class libraries which have been outlined above. Not all of these classes require an instance definition.
Instances can be defined for User Interface objects and Package Man-

Exhibit 18.4   MacroScope architecture.

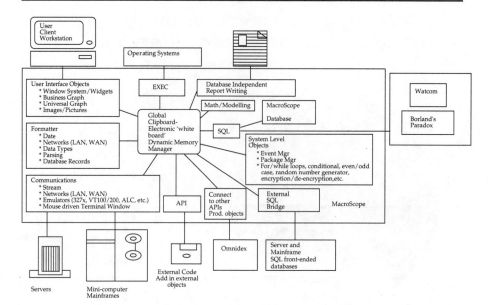

agers. Package Managers are methods which are not tied to any user interface. They are activated by message rather than mouse click or touch.

– Inheritance/specialization.

Inheritance is achieved in two areas. The first is in user interfaces. A recessed "motif" looking window, for example, inherits a rectangular window and four lines which reflect recessed highlighting. The second area is the inheritance of methods. This is illustrated substantially through the use of Package Managers. For example, an HPPCL printer driver object was written in MacroScope rather than underlying C code. Foundation methods support picking font, their size, serif/sans-serif, italicized, boldness value, etc. These package managers were inherited to produce month-at-a-glance calendars in any size, business graphs, etc. This layer was inherited again to produce time management output, reports to generate, and so forth.

– Methods/messages.

Methods within MacroScope are described via messages to user-defined and system level objects. System level objects are outlined in the diagram above.

– Virtual methods/polymorphism.

Package Managers support virtual methods. MacroScope facilitates both static and dynamic polymorphism.

ADVANCED OO FUNCTIONALITY
– Persistent objects.

Developers have the ability to create object persistence within the application where applicable. This is achieved by using database or file system structures which are interpreted at application load. Throughout the execution of an application, object persistence is automatically maintained.

– Dynamic class/method generation.

This is supported by the Graphical Development tool and its ability to create messages on the fly and immediately execute and store them. The tool is supported by underlying messages, which allows developers to pass message/method descriptions, have them compiled on the fly, and instantly executed.

– Constraint programming.

Constraints have been built into the base MacroScope object classes and are designed in such a way to allow end developers to manipulate classes in conjunction with each other to create the desired constraints for systems and new application oriented object classes.

EXTENDED PROGRAMMING ENVIRONMENT
– Functional programming.

Developers create functional components through the use of Package Managers. MacroScope developed objects work with existing functional technical building blocks. Developers work with functional elements. Underneath, messages are C code objects which interface with technologies on a procedural (API) level. Procedure level programming is hidden from MacroScope developers.

DEVELOPMENT ENVIRONMENT
– Graphical developer interface.

MacroScope includes graphical point and click development tools. These tools have been written using MacroScope and therefore can be incorporated with live applications for modification, or can be used to create applications from the beginning.

– Interpreted internal language.

MacroScope is compiled and interpreted. MacroScope is compiled producing data structures which represent the definition of applications (i.e., high level op-code). These data structures are interpreted, at very high speed. MacroScope allows developers to send ASCII definition code to system level objects for on-the-fly compilation and immediate execution. This provides facilities identical to those found in Lisp and Prolog without the overhead and extensive performance degradation of garbage collection.

– Graphical browsers.

Graphical browsing is supported by Graphical Programming Tools. The modification to MacroScope's database to allow a field type of messages, allows SQL to also manage objects and browse libraries.

– Automatic links to databases.

In addition to an internal database, links to external databases have been added. Currently hooks into server and mainframe SQL front-ended databases (e.g. Sybase, Oracle, Ingres, DB2, IMS, VSAM, IBM flat files), as well as Paradox, Watcom SQL, and Omnidex, are available as object classes to developers. The developer simply sends an SQL message to the appropriate object.

– Internal/external class libraries.

In addition to base classes provided with MacroScope, an application program interface has been provided which allows developers to add their own external C-based classes.

– Class libraries interpreted.

Through the use of the graphical development tools, class libraries can be read in, viewed, and altered as desired. Creation of new libraries with user defined constraints to limit look-and-feel can also be developed on-the-fly for immediate interpretation.

– Editors, indexers, consistency checkers.

Templates have been designed for use with the Brief Editor allowing developers to simply fill in required information. MacroScope's compilers check for errors which have occurred in the definition of the application. At run-time several debugging options can be invoked in order to trap execution errors.

– Graphical tool for user interface development.

Written in MacroScope.

– Tools for target operating system interface layout available.

The run-time interpreter is available across major platforms (DOS, MS Windows, OS/2, Macintosh) and is designed to interpret instance files across all platforms without application modification, insuring functional integrity throughout. Any interface directly with the operating system can be achieved through the EXEC class environment.

STORAGE MANAGEMENT

– Repository available.

A collection of utilities and useful library facilities have been created to assist developers and provide commonly requested objects. A Bulletin Board System is provided for easy access to these and allows developers to make available additional facilities of interest.

– Version control available.

Objective uses commercially available Revision Control software which is used to manage C-based class libraries, MacroScope-developed objects, and documentation. In addition, an internal check is provided to insure that compiled binary code is compatible with current run-time executables.

CODE GENERATION

– Language code generated.

Graphics tools and editors are used to generate MacroScope code. This is compiled into a binary internal op-code representation.

– Compiled code generated.

The compiler generates internal binary representation equivalent to a high level op-code definition with which run-time objects configure themselves and act upon for execution requests ("execute this SQL statement").

PROJECT LIFE CYCLE

Analysis and Design

Before Global MIS, Thomas Cook had little experience with object-oriented approaches. The Thomas Cook Group had considered modifying one of a number of existing national MI systems to provide the multinational capability of consolidation. However this option was rejected because it would have resulted in:

1. Little, if any improvement in delivery timescale;

2. A less flexible system developed in a less advanced environment;

3. A shorter system life.

Development on an IBM mainframe was considered but rejected due to delivery timescales, cost, and inflexibility.

According to Will Thornton-Reid, Manager IT, Global Travel Development at the Thomas Cook Group:

Objective International presented a proposal which, using their MacroScope tools and development methodology, provided functionality, flexibility, high quality GUI, and delivery in a very accelerated timescale.

Global MIS was designed, developed and delivered in five months.

BENEFITS

Benefits gained from the system include:

- Low cost development through object reusability and easy maintenance;

- Simplified development, maintenance, and enhancement due to object-oriented, (highly modular) design;

- Minimized costs and elapsed time for integration of all market data, and with reduced disturbance, by not having to dictate changes to the existing systems;

- Reduced costs by extending payback of existing systems;

- Required less training due to intuitive GUI and dynamic help and on-line help system making use of "hot spots" allowing messages to be broadcast to the user;

- Offered early benefits due to speed of implementation;

- Reduced complexity of accessing data held in multiple systems in different world markets, increasing significantly the source of data and speed of access;

- Improved user appreciation by enhancing the usability of a complex reporting process that produces high quality graphical and textual reports;

- Enabled Thomas Cook to provide a unique service to the corporate travel market, supporting extended market penetration;

- Reinforced Thomas Cook's corporate image to clients.

- Increased sales by providing a powerful new marketing tool for the corporate sales department.

CONCLUSIONS

Will Thornton-Reid is impressed that such a valuable system could be developed so quickly:

> A very impressive demonstration system and user on-line system have also been developed to help support our customers' and partners' global business aims. All the customers who have seen these systems have been extremely impressed with their quality and functionality, further enhancing Thomas Cook's image as a user of up-to-date high technology.

CHAPTER 19

Application Description

LINKUP

Linkup was developed by Westinghouse Savannah River Company (WSRC) in HyperCard which most people (including its vendors) fail to associate with object-oriented technology. While significantly limited, HyperCard is in fact an OO development tool, as the following description demonstrates.

STATEMENT OF THE PROBLEM

The motivation to create Linkup arises from the following scenario:

> Every so often, employees receive new documents because they have been placed on a distribution list. Most of the documents give no outward indication of what part of their contents may pertain to the recipient. In one case, an employee received a thick document, and having no great desire to read it, placed it on the shelf. Several weeks later, the employee received a call as to why certain reports had not been submitted in accordance with a statement buried somewhere in the middle of the document.

Linkup was created to extract structure and relationships from textual data and to deliver it in a form that improves the user's ability to search and browse the data.

The goal at the outset of the project was to improve the communication of information throughout the company, both from management down to employees and between employees of different organizations within WSRC. Also sought was a reduction in the amount of time spent looking for information, or in trying to determine whether the information provided is useful or applicable to particular users.

In the view of the project team, people tend to be uncomfortable with large amounts of information. Broken down into chunks, or objects, information becomes more manageable because people can ignore details and concentrate on finding which objects are relevant. In addition, data captured as objects can be combined in a number of ways to express meaningful relationships.

SOLUTION: LINKUP

Linkup is a information delivery system which provides widespread user access to a variety of data sources. Applications for the system are created by analyzing existing data for structure and relationships, and then using the results of the analysis to create objects, which are implemented as cards in HyperCard stacks. The stacks allow users to search the data, to view it at different levels of abstraction and to move from one object to another based on the relationships identified during the analysis phase. The data analysis and the stack creation are performed by separate programs.

Exhibit 19.1 lists Linkup's major components. According to programmer John Krieger, Linkup represents an atypical OO solution because it does not use traditional classes, methods or inheritance. All objects are represented in terms of cards and buttons, and scripts associated with the objects stand in the place of methods. Some examples of objects represented in Linkup include employees, organizations, and procedures.

Exhibit 19.1   System components.

	Hardware	*Software*
Interface	Macintosh	HyperCard
Core Code	N/A	C
Database	N/A	N/A
Development Environment	Macintosh	HyperCard

Linkup consists largely of scripts divided into two primary functions: creation of stacks and interface support. The first set of scripts reads the input data, creates the appropriate cards, and establishes buttons which link the cards. The second set of scripts handles user input such as mouse clicks. The size of the Hypertalk software is about 500K.

The software that prepares data for reading by HyperCard has been variously implemented in Fortran, Lisp, and C. Use of a particular language has usually been determined by the environment where the source data is stored. In any case, the purpose of the software is to generate files expressed in an internal markup language.

One of the uses of Linkup has been to integrate data extracts from several mainframe databases into a single system. The system, called TOPDOWN, gives Macintosh users access to data on the 19,000 individuals and 2,000 organizations which make up the company. Upon entering the system, the user sees a listing of all first level organizations. Similar to an outlining tool, the user can choose to see the next level of detail for an organization, or the user can go directly to the organization's card. The outliner acts as a browser, and the cards provide detail as an object inspector would.

A card for a given organization has links to both the superior and subordinate organizations, as well as a listing of assigned employees. Each employee name is linked to a separate card containing information such as the employee's location, phone number, manager, and so forth. Employee cards can also be located either by reference to an index or by textual search. One benefit of TOPDOWN has been the "visualizing" of personnel databases so that inconsistencies can be identified and corrected. The primary benefit for users has been the ability to locate people quickly in the context of the organization where they work.

Linkup has also been used to deliver electronic documents, such as the company policy manuals. In this scheme, the cards in a stack represent the basic components of a document. The browser provides an overview of the document contents, and the index provides listings of cards which pertain to a particular subject. Links between cards allow the user to follow cross-references to other documents, and a glossary provides short definitions of acronyms or unfamiliar terms. As with the personnel data, the analysis phase has identified a number of inconsistencies, and users have benefited from greater access to the manual set.

Exhibit 19.2 shows Linkup's user interface, including a reader window, a help window, and a collection of function buttons (the "palette"). The reader is displaying a table of contents. The arrows in the left margin indicate whether more levels of detail exist for a given topic. Clicking on a topic displays the corresponding card. The messages in the help window change as the user moves the mouse over various areas of the reader. Buttons on the palette provide access to search, navigation, and extended help functions.

Exhibit 19.3 shows the text of a card. The top of the card shows specific information about this part of the manual, and buttons at the bottom provide access to adjacent cards and to the table of contents. References are represented by underlined areas, and clicking on a reference displays the corresponding card or figure. On this screen the pointer is shown over an acronym ("CQF") which has been expanded for the user in the help window.

Exhibit 19.2   Linkup user interface.

reader

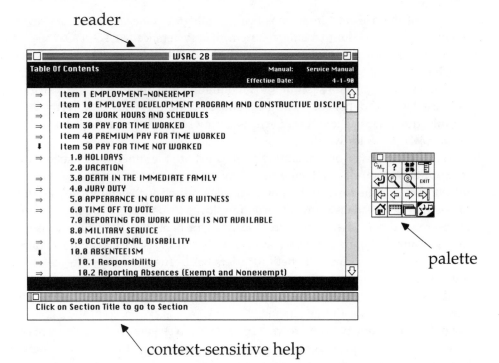

palette

context-sensitive help

Exhibit 19.3   Card text.

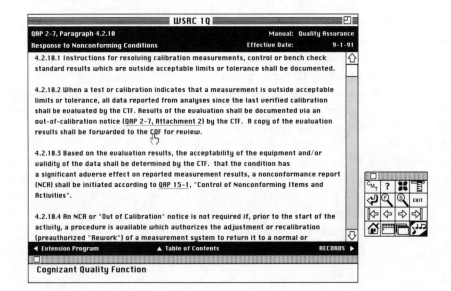

PROJECT LIFE CYCLE

Analysis and Design

WSRC is probably similar to many companies in that its employees are working with OO technology, but a "true" OO application has yet to be deployed. Some of the earliest OO work at WSRC was done in Lisp environments, although most of their people are now using C + +. Linkup was created because Phil Ames, the project manager, saw capabilities in the Lisp environment that he thought would be more desirable if they were available on a Macintosh.

To sell the proposed solution, the team found that the most important factor was showing data which was relevant to their customers. For example, a person interested in an on-line policy manual could not always grasp the benefits of the technology from seeing an on-line computer manual, even though the capabilities involved were the same.

Development

The initial development of Linkup was undertaken by Messrs. Ames and Krieger, using rapid prototyping. The first prototype was completed in the space of one calendar month based on the capabilities of a system Krieger had developed in the Symbolics Lisp environment. The test data for the first prototype was taken from a document that was being prepared for publication by another group.

The project team chose HyperCard for three reasons. First, they wanted an environment that provided a straightforward mapping of document components to objects. Second, they wanted to be able to develop prototypes quickly, especially in regard to building user interfaces. Third, the Apple Macintosh was their target platform, and at the time, HyperCard could be freely distributed to anyone who had a Macintosh.

After a few initial successes with small data sets, they encountered some problems of scale. They found that larger data sets took longer and longer to process, occasionally breaking some parts of the software based on faulty assumptions. They also found that some performance problems were due to the non-obvious cost of some costly operations in HyperCard.

Using one particularly large data set, they were successful in "shaking down" the system to eliminate several performance bottlenecks. In one case, they reduced processing time from four hours to thirteen minutes. Eric Sherbine joined the team at this point to continue extending the capabilities of the software, and Jack Roberts later optimized both the interface software and the internal markup format.

Deployment

Linkup applications have been deployed in two ways. First, selected applications have been distributed directly to users; second, general applications have been made available on network servers. The first case usually involves specialized data which does not require frequent updates, and where the users prefer the improved performance available through local access to the software.

The main deployment problem has been the poor performance of HyperCard over a network. Running on a Macintosh-based Appleshare server, the team found HyperCard to be unacceptably slow. A major networking company is currently addressing the incompatibility of its software with HyperCard, and the team's experience using a Sun server has yielded inconsistent performance.

To date, they have offered no formal user training for Linkup. They have provided both informal training and user documentation, but the project team is too small to offer a complete training program. There are currently about 100 users of Linkup, and as the software gains additional users, internal computer training groups are expected to add Linkup to their curricula.

Maintenance

A number of problems were revealed through user testing, so most of the recent maintenance of the software has consisted of attempts to enhance general performance. The team has not added any significant new capabilities to the basic application since it was deployed. They are continuing work on an interface that will allow data administrators to update their own data without requiring the services of a programmer. Meanwhile, they are performing periodic updates for specific applications.

BENEFITS

Overall, they see the benefits of Linkup as divided into three catagories: data management, productivity, and cost reduction.

The primary benefit in the data management area is an enhanced view of data as a corporate resource. Previously, data has been collected for specific purposes, such as accounting and publishing, without regard to the alternative uses. As a result, the quality of the data might be adequate for its intended application, but insufficient for other applications. Their efforts to deliver electronic versions of documents and organization charts have identified inconsistencies in corporate data and have spawned several ongoing quality improvement programs.

They see productivity improvements as a consequence of improved access to information. Any employee with a policy question and access to a computer can find the specific parts of each manual that pertain to a given subject. Before or after attending a meeting, an employee can "read up" on the participants. Employees have also used the electronic organization chart to search for people doing similar work in other divisions of the company. Centralized maintenance removes the burden of updates and ensures that users have access to the latest information.

Costs are being reduced through decreased requirements for creating, maintaining, and distributing paper copies of documents. While they do not expect to abolish paper, they do expect to serve more users with less paper, and with significantly fewer people than the several hundred dedicated to drawing organization charts and tracking paper copies of manuals. Exact figures are not yet available but savings in the two areas mentioned are estimated to be one to two million dollars per year.

Here's how John Krieger sums up the benefits:

> The greatest benefit from deploying Linkup applications has been improved user access to information. Most of our employees are unaware of the information available to them because our company has lacked an effective vehicle for communicating it. While our mainframe systems are perceived as inflexible and cumbersome, users often respond to Linkup demonstrations by saying, "When can I get that?"
>
> The Linkup software is a testimony to what can be accomplished by a small development group using a moderately powerful programming environment. Despite its limited concept of objects and methods, HyperCard has allowed us to accomplish projects in months, as opposed to estimates given us by other groups that place the development time at several years each.
>
> The ability to reuse our Linkup software has allowed us to develop new prototypes in record time. In addition, since the applications share a common interface, users who are familiar with one application can take advantage of the consistency and spend more time concentrating on the new features of an application.
>
> Although our users probably deserve some kind of formal training, they have been able to start using Linkup applications with minimal instruction. Some of the credit for reduced training time goes to sound interface design, but credit is also due to the design of the tools available in the development environment.

CONCLUSIONS

John Krieger puts Linkup into company-wide perspective:

> Among ourselves, we have referred to Linkup as "the poor man's database." What Linkup provides is an intuitive means of delivering information without affecting the way the data is maintained. While we deliver information we are trying to raise "object awareness" so that our company is prepared for the inevitable transition to object technology.
>
> One lesson from this project and previous projects is that OO applications require some tuning to achieve optimum performance. While OO development environments often provide a service by hiding low-level details from the imple-

mentor, they may do a disservice if seemingly simple operations turn out to be costly in practice.

The single most useful piece of advice we can provide is to choose a delivery environment which will reach a large percentage of potential users. Some OO development environments require special hardware or software that may complicate delivery of applications. The desirable features of a development environment should not outweigh the practicality of delivering a finished system.

Domain: Medicine

Unlike the software development industry, where people expect software innovation, many are surprised that the medical industry is also at the front of software innovation. It is even more surprising when you consider that many of the most interesting software products in the medical area have been developed by doctors rather than by professional programmers. Of course, there are several good reasons why medical people have proved so innovative. First, the medical industry has been under very significant pressure to contain costs. Government and private agencies have provided generous funding to individuals and groups that have suggested ways to improve health care productivity. And, of course, as in many industries, new computer applications have inspired many with the hope that they can provide productivity increases. Additional factors include the highly technical nature of medical practice, and the very significant power of the end users, many of whom are physicians. Companies may force clerical and even middle managers to use systems that are unfriendly and difficult, but it is very hard to get bright, highly stressed individuals like physicians to use systems that add to the difficulties of their work.

The combination of the need and the high standards demanded of many medical systems has resulted in an interesting phenomena. Physicians, like engineers in some other industries, have shown what can be done when bright nonprogrammers adopt new technologies to create domain-specific decision-support systems. Physician-developers have been at the forefront in identifying user-friendly development tools and using them to create some of the most innovative, user-friendly decision-support systems. In the early 1980s, physician-developers played a leading role in the development of some of the most powerful expert systems, and they are currently playing an active role in the application of object-oriented techniques to medical problems.

There are two examples included in this section. One is clearly a medical example. The second has many different uses, including medical applications. Both illustrate the use of object technology for creating graphical interfaces. Since both these applications are, in fact, meta-tools designed to facilitate the development of other applications, they also illustrate the reuse of code and the very powerful ideas involved in class libraries and the specialization of inherited code. Each application also illustrates the power of object techniques to manipulate simultaneously many different data types.

Helios is a software engineering environment that was developed to assist hospital software developers in the generation of hospital information systems. The project was supported by several groups operating within the framework of the EEC and led by Dr. François-Cristophe Jean at Broussais University Hospital in Paris. Using Helios, European physicians can now create information systems that gather and display a wide variety of patient data.

General Electric's LYMB is a computer graphics animation system that facilitates the easy visualization of data and experiments. Like Helios, LYMB is a meta-tool that can be used by other developers to create specific simulation systems. LYMB has been used to create 2 and 3D medical imaging systems, and it has also been used to create systems to help TV viewers visualize golf games and to help engineers visualize a jet engine's performance.

As computing becomes increasingly visual and as simulations become routine in conducting research, object technology will increasingly dominate scientific research and medical applications.

CHAPTER 20

Application Description

LYMB

STATEMENT OF THE PROBLEM

The Computer Graphics and Systems Program is a focused research group within General Electric's Corporate Research and Development (GE-CRD) that develops algorithms and applications serving a variety of GE businesses. Internal customers include GE Medical Systems, GE Aircraft Engine, GE Aerospace, and NBC. Most of their efforts have graphics or user interface aspects.

LYMB originated in 1984 as a graphics animation system to allow scientists and engineers to see the results of their analyses and experiments. Until that time, users had relied on computer scientists and graphics engineers to create custom applications to visualize their data. This was seen as an opportunity to experiment with what was then a new and untested technology.

SOLUTION: LYMB

LYMB is an object-oriented development environment (available under license from GE-CRD). Its purpose is to create general-purpose or custom software applications where there are significant requirements of graphics-based user interfaces, visualization, and computer graphics. LYMB is organized into a set of Core classes of objects and Libraries of objects that are aimed at application development.

LYMB's core objects are:

- Parser, Message Passing
- Basic Arithmetic and Control objects
- Unix Programming Tools
- Class Generator
- HP widget set (user interface)
- VOGLE Renderer

LYMB's Library objects are:

- User Interface (X Windows, Motif)
- Visualization
- Graphics and Geometric Modellers
- Animation
- Renderers (GL, starbase, phigs, vogle, hoops, KGL)
- Numerical
- Integration with External Software

LYMB consists of classes, a message handler, and a parser. The classes are written in C and manipulated at run-time using the parser. LYMB applications are written by grouping LYMB statements in script files that create instances from classes and manipulate these instances.

Each LYMB class is defined by a C structure that contains elements representing each instance variable, meta information about the object, and the object's method table. LYMB has two types of objects: classes and instances. Classes exist at system start-up while instances are created during an application's execution. Classes serve primarily as templates for instance creation, also holding information available to all instances of a class. Each class is implemented in a single C source file. Within that file, all methods (C procedures) and instance variables (C structures) are declared static. Exhibit 20.1 shows the major components of LYMB.

All access to an object's state is through the LYMB message handler, msg. This central dispatcher is called directly by class developers using the msg send procedure or indirectly by application developers through the parser. Msg matches message strings to method addresses through an object's method dictionary. LYMB implements behavior inheritance by first searching an object's methods

Exhibit 20.1   Current system components.

	Hardware	Software
Interface	UNIX Workstations	X Windows, Motif, HP Widget Set
Core Code	UNIX Workstations	C (C++ in future)
Database	N/A	N/A
Development Environment	UNIX Workstations	LYMB Scripting Language C Classes, Meta Classes

and, if the search fails, proceeds to that object's super class. All LYMB objects eventually inherit behavior from a class called *Object*. *Object* implements messages that are useful to all objects in the system such as printing an object's state and getting help about an object. Each object has a Unix main page describing its instance variables, messages and a sample script. The LYMB parser implements a simple syntax with one statement, which allows the creation and manipulation of instances.

Class Libraries   Over 500 classes are available to applications in 30 class libraries. Core classes provide a common kernel for applications. These classes include scalars, strings, collections, vectors, logics, and actions. Actions logically group LYMB statements that are executed when the object receives a *tick!* message.

The animation classes, which control the location and appearance of actors over time, are still heavily used in most LYMB applications. LYMB's animation model is based on the traditional notion of movie production. Actor objects represent the position, orientation, and visible properties of the characters in the animation. Camera and light objects model their physical counterparts. Users choreograph the actors with scenes and cues. A scene controls the execution of multiple cues which, if active, send LYMB statements to the parser. A keyframe object can control the smooth interpolation of any instance variable of any object in the system. The user identifies certain "key" times, messages, and values for an object and the keyframe object automatically generates data, splines, and cues that will smoothly vary the values over the specified time interval.

An abstract "renderer" class implements a portable rendering protocol. The specifics of rendering for a given hardware platform are carried out by subclasses that are hardware-specific. For example, LYMB has a "gl" class for Silicon Graphics workstations that uses SGI's gl library to do rendering. The DECstation uses PHIGS and the HP uses Starbase.

Over 70 visualization and data manipulation classes exist to display the results of 2D and 3D analyses. Reader, filter, and modeler classes are combined in networks to process data before viewing with the renderer classes. Readers import data from files or other external sources and convert it to a canonical form. Readers exist for many standard file formats including netCDF, PLOT3D, MOVIE.BYU, and GEOMOD. Filters transform the canonical data with classes such as isosurface generation, streamline creation, and triangle decimation. Modelers convert the canonical forms to displayable objects.

Since modern applications require window interfaces, LYMB has X11 and Motif class libraries. X11 data structures such as windows, pixmaps, and graphics contexts exist as objects and the procedures that manipulate them are accessible as methods. Motif widgets map one-to-one to LYMB classes with callback implemented as LYMB actions that can be specified and modified at run-time.

Advanced Features   LYMB provides several advanced features to aid class development and enhance application functionality. A LYMB class generator object automatically generates the C code necessary to create a LYMB class. This object, using LYMB syntax, takes a specification of a class's instance variables and messages to produce C code that implements inheritance, the method dictionary and methods to modify and access an object's state. The developer need only supply C code for those methods that implement object-specific behavior.

Users can also create LYMB classes using a utility that converts Object Model Diagrams created with GE-CRD's OMTool into LYMB class C code. The user graphically constructs object hierarchies and associations. This rich notation also describes the instance variables and methods for each class.

Although most classes in LYMB are implemented in C, a meta class object provides application developers with a facility to build classes at run-time. The resulting classes are often required as data holders or classes that have simple behavior specific to an application. For example, in a command and control application, a ship class may be needed that is really an actor with some additional properties such as heading and speed. When creating a C class implementation, the developer can use the meta class to subclass from actor and add the few additional features for the application.

A LYMB process object permits multiple LYMB processes to communicate using a network protocol. The communicating LYMBs can reside on different workstations of different manufacture. Marshaling of large data sets between the processes uses industry standard XDR protocols.

The X Intrinsics class supports a recording facility that keeps track of user interactions within a window application. These interactions are stored in a file that can be replayed later, on either the same workstation or on another vendor platform. The recording is used for quality control testing, live-action help, and session recording on videotape.

A Motif Resource Manager class converts Motif UIL created by external programs, such as XDesigner or the Builder Xcessory, into LYMB scripts. Users can graphically lay out user interfaces with these commercial layout systems, convert them to LYMB, and then gain access to LYMB's interpretive environment.

LYMB interfaces with a variety of external software packages. A semi-automatic procedure is in place to create "wrapper classes" for such interfaces. For example, the wrapper class implements one-to-one mapping between library routines, such as the Numerical Recipes library, and wrapper methods.

A Network Editor is available to graphically define the dependencies among process or data objects. The resulting network can then be used to execute, including concurrent processes, the logical sequence of links to objects in the network. Exhibit 20.2 summarizes some of the major functionalities of LYMB.

Exhibit 20.2   Summary of major functionality.

LYMB Functionality

3D Graphics
- Lights
- Cameras
- Actors
- Renderers (gl, phigs, starbase, X11, 4010 Tek, postscript, interleaf)
- Assemblies
- Primitives
- Transformation

Animation
- scenes
- cues
- loops
- recorders

User Interface
- Xlib
- Xt
- Motif
- HP widgets
- Athena widgets
- X plotting

Modellers
- GEOMOD
- MOVIE.BYU
- marching cubes
- spheres
- cones
- cubes
- cylinders
- lines
- golf

Visualization
- geometry
- vector fields
- streamlines, ribbons, and tubes
- cut planes
- iso-surfaces
- line contours
- 0D, 1D, 2D, and 3D probes
- filters & network
- structured grids
- unstructured grids
- volume data
- unstructured point sets
- fully transient data

Unix Interface
- asynchronous and synchronous shells
- file I/O
- signal handler
- network communication
- environment variables

Data Interface
- PLOT3D
- netCDF
- AVS
- PHOENICS
- ANSYS
- ASCII

Miscellaneous
- scalars
- vectors
- strings
- arithmetic
- logic
- looping
- conditional execution
- procedures
- recursion

PROJECT LIFE CYCLE

Dr. Peter Meenan managed the overall LYMB project. While many developers continue to work on LYMB, two of the key people responsible for concept design and development were Bill Lorensen and Dr. Boris Yamrom. Significant design and initial implementation help was also provided by Michelle Barry, currently with Star Technologies, and Dan McLachlan, now with Kubota, Inc.

Analysis and Design

No commercial, portable, object-oriented systems were available in 1984, so the team decided to implement an OO system in C. They added object-oriented constructs to standard C by using the C preprocessor and a few simple coding conventions. Run-time message passing and a parser provided the dynamic framework required to do computer animation. After initial success with the animation system, called OSCAR (Object-oriented SCene AnimatoR), they added class libraries to LYMB, extending its functionality to a variety of visualization and user interface applications.

Development

Initially, the project team turned to Booch's methodology, which they describe in one of their internal publications:

> At first glance, Booch's approach seems attractive. One just writes down a description of the system to be modeled, underlines the nouns (these become objects), then the verbs (these become operations), and translates the design into Ada. But he has not described a design methodology, giving only guidelines for translating a design into an object-oriented implementation. Although his guidelines are useful for that step, moving from the problem definition step to the informal strategy is the most difficult step of the design process.

The team created its own six step methodology:

1. Identify the data abstractions for each subsystem.
   These data abstractions will be the objects of the system.

2. Identify the attributes for each abstraction.
   The attributes become the instance variables for each object.

3. Identify the operations for each abstraction.
   The operations are the methods for each object.

4. Identify the communication between objects.
   This step defines the messages that objects can send to each other.

5. Test the design scenarios.
   The designer should write a scenario of messages for each requirement in the system specification.

6. Apply inheritance where appropriate.
   Once some objects have been designed, common data and operations often surface; common instance variables can be combined into a class.

From the first 25 classes developed for animation, the 30 LYMB class libraries now have over 500 classes to support applications in scientific visualization, image processing, user interfaces, and computer graphics. LYMB can be ported to any UNIX workstation and currently runs on Sun3/4, Silicon Graphics, IBM RS6000, DEC, and Hewlett Packard systems. Using class libraries for X11 and Motif, LYMB window-based applications can also run unaltered on these systems. A graphics rendering abstraction permits LYMB to access vendor-optimized rendering libraries.

Deployment

Dozens of applications have been developed with LYMB by various organizations within GE, including:

VISAGE is the largest of these applications. VISAGE (VISualization Animation and Graphics Environment) is a scientific visualization tool designed to manipulate structured and unstructured grid and point set data. It supports several visualization techniques including 0D, 1D, and 2D probes, streamtubes, hedgehogs, isosurfaces, cut planes, transparency, and vector field display. VISAGE relies on the animation, rendering, and data representation classes to present a turnkey application to scientists and engineers doing analyses such as computational fluid mechanics, heat transfer, or structural analysis. Exhibit 20.3 shows a VISAGE screen with Motif user interface and graphical results of the computational fluid dynamics analysis. The object is an annular combustor for a jet engine. The planar region is a vertical cut through the data with flow density mapped as color.

The GOLF GREEN VISUALIZATION system enhances a TV viewer's perception of the complex topography of a golf putting green and demonstrates how that topography affects the trajectory of a putted ball. As a spectator watching a golf tournament on TV, it is nearly impossible to appreciate the difficulty that a golfer faces when putting the ball. This is due to the sun's diffuse overhead lighting and limitations on the position of TV cameras.

Exhibit 20.3   Sample VISAGE screen.

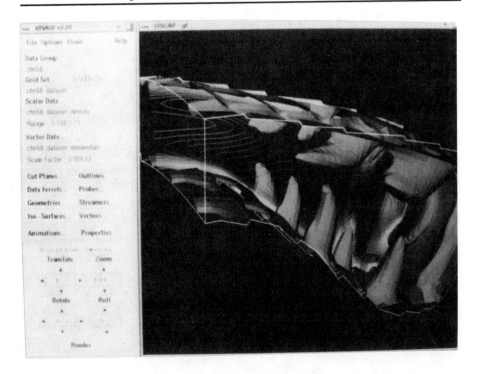

Exhibit 20.4   Typical View-a-Putt images.

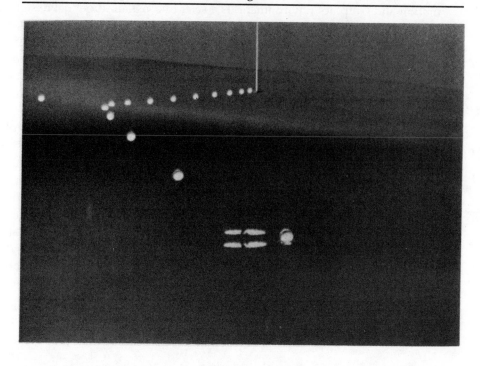

LYMB models the actual golf green using polygons and manipulates camera and light objects to enhance the green topography. Differential equation solver classes calculate the trajectory of a perfect putt from the golfer's ball to the hole. The system was used successfully in an NBC televised LPGA tournament in July 1991. Exhibit 20.4 shows a typical image from View-a-Putt. The transparent vertical plane through the ball and the pin helps the viewer understand how much the putt will break.

VIVA is an image-processing tool for viewing industrial and medical 2D and 3D image data, such as is generated by CT and MRI systems. VIVA users, through a LYMB Motif interface, can display multiple images simultaneously, control the mapping between image values and displayed pixels, interactively reformat data along arbitrary planes and display 3D surface renditions of internal anatomy or parts. Exhibit 20.5 shows a sample VIVA screen with image-processing and display capabilities. The four images in the center represent computed tomography, positron emission tomography (PET), and two 3D surface displays of a turbine blade. The various pop-ups allow the user to

Exhibit 20.5   Sample VIVA screen.

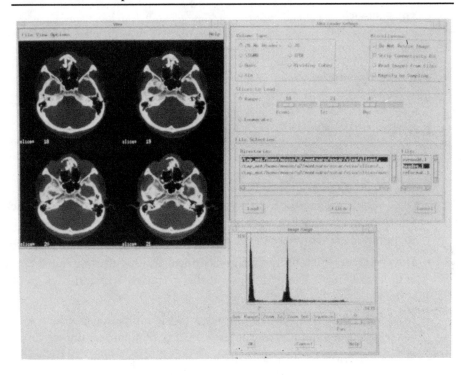

control the placement of the images and their colors. The graph at the lower right shows a histogram of intensity values for the computed tomography image.

BENEFITS

To Dr. Meenan the main benefits of LYMB are its portability and the reusability of its libraries. He also emphasizes the capability to do rapid prototyping which LYMB provides. According to Dr. Meenan:

> Marketing is an important part of any organization that builds products. We often build demonstrations or prototypes to illustrate visualization techniques or apply algorithms to new applications. The LYMB run-time interpreter lets us do this prototyping very quickly without having to go through the conventional edit-compile-link-execute cycle.
>
> Recently we were asked by a GE component to build a shipboard user interface for command and control to investigate inter-control-room communications.

The interface runs on two separate workstations, simulating two separate control consoles. Actions on one console are reported to the other for verification. Two LYMB application developers put this prototype together in less than one week. The resulting screens presented a realistic representation of the control consoles. Interprocess communication was accomplished using the LYMB distributed processing protocol. This application used the Motif and X11 class libraries. No new classes were developed.

CONCLUSIONS

A paper by the development team cites the following conclusions:

- The object-oriented approach has resulted in major benefits for the research team, making it more productive and allowing them to respond quickly. The sharing and reuse of class libraries also creates an environment of team cooperation and software development that benefits multiple projects.

- The abstraction step of the design is critical and requires the most amount of time and effort. The path taken at this point will drive the design of the system.

- Applying the data abstraction process to the animation production cycle has resulted in a natural user interface using familiar terminology.

- The object-oriented approach allows the natural partition of complex systems into manageable pieces. No single object is complex, but the system as a whole can deal with the complexity of the process being modeled.

- The system is less fragile than others written previously. Objects can be modified and added without fear of breaking the system.

CHAPTER 21

Application Description

HELIOS

The twelve-nation European Economic Community has become an important advocate of new and emerging technologies, with major investments in programs that explore advanced solutions to a variety of medical and scientific problems—many of which are based on object-oriented technology.

One example is HELIOS, a program to develop an object-oriented software engineering environment for a new generation of multimedia hospital applications.

STATEMENT OF THE PROBLEM

With an extensive background in building medical applications with traditional databases (both relational and semantic) and tools (third generation languages such as Fortran and C), the developers of HELIOS knew that building a new application means re-programming standard pieces of code that are found in every application. This re-programming can represent as much as 80% of the total programming effort. With traditional techniques, reusing previous work is very difficult, which is why they turned to object technology and specifically to an object database management system.

Pr. Patrice Degoulet, head of the Medical Informatics Department at Broussais University Hospital in Paris, frames the problem like this:

> Efforts needed to develop software increase non-linearly with the size and complexity of the programs to be achieved. This is particularly true in the medical domain where developments, such as Ward Information Systems, might represent several hundred person-years of effort. Furthermore, medical systems are faced with changing requirements, motivated by fast growing technologies. Thus, systems must be both open and reshapable in various ways to take new constraints easily into consideration. For these reasons, it is important to provide medical application engineers with a set of tools which simplifies their jobs, encourages collaborative work, improves productivity and enhances the quality of the generated applications.

The problem was to create an environment that could streamline the development of distributed multimedia medical applications. In fact, the different partners involved in the HELIOS project had a great deal of experience building medical applications, but had used a lot of ad-hoc tools that didn't allow easy reuse of the previously built parts.

Medicine is a field where techniques are constantly evolving. Because of this, they wanted an open framework, able to accept new "pluggable" components dedicated to the management of particular aspects of medical information. Dividing the whole environment into separate software components federated by a "software bus," called the Helios Unification Bus, allows for easy replacement of one component by another without having to recompile or reconfigure.

The target application for the HELIOS environment is a multimedia hospital ward information system (WIS), constituted by a network of workstations gathering patient-centered information in a specific medical discipline. HELIOS's current specialty is cardiology with an emphasis on heart surgery follow-up and high blood pressure management, because these are two fields that rely heavily on the use of images and complex data types. In a typical cardiac ward, information concerning the management of a heart transplant patient might be available in various locations throughout the hospital.

SOLUTION: HELIOS

The Ward Information System, built with HELIOS is designed to bring all of the information together, regardless of its format, in one convenient place at decision-making time.

The HELIOS architecture consists of three main parts: the Kernel, the Unification Bus, and the Services. Exhibit 21.1 shows the basic HELIOS architecture.

THE KERNEL includes the GemStone-based information system, interface manager, and an analysis and design environment. The information system is the data repository for both development and run-time, storing two kinds of objects: software objects which store the source code produced by developers when building medical applications, and application objects, which are pre-defined objects commonly used in medical applications. There are four classes of medical application objects:

- Actors, such as physicians, nurses, patients.
- Activities such as care providing, data acquisition.
- Concepts, such as sign, symptom, diagnosis, and
- Entity Representations, such as free text, images, results tables, sorted lists, charts.

Exhibit 21.1   HELIOS architecture.

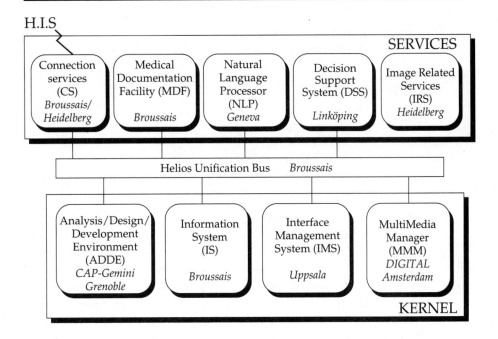

The HELIOS UNIFICATION BUS allows for the exchange of data between components and handles the distribution aspects of data communication, providing for easy integration of new software components. A high-level communication service is used at run-time to pass messages between different software components.

The SERVICES, a collection of toolboxes linked to the Kernel via the Unification Bus to give additional functionality to developers and end-users for manipulating the medical objects. The first service to be implemented was an Image Related Services, which allow on-screen display and simulated manipulation of images such as x-rays, histograms, and CT scans. Additional services, such as natural language processing, decision support, and integrated management of video and audio information, are planned. Exhibit 21.2 shows the basic components of HELIOS.

BASIC OO FUNCTIONALITY

All basic OO functionalities are used in HELIOS. It currently uses single inheritance. Persistence of objects is done through the use of an object-oriented database, GemStone. Special focus is put on message-passing facilities, extending the capabilities provided by the OODBMS. Method

Exhibit 21.2   System components.

	Hardware	Software
Interface	RISC and x terminals	OSF/Motif x Windows
Core Code	RISC	C++, Opal, Object Prolog
Database	RISC	GemStone
Development Environment	DECSTATION 5000/240 (ULTRIX)	DECFuse, Servio

selectors are always defined and stored in the database classes even if the body of the method (effector) is stored and compiled in a remote software component. In this case the message sent to the class is forwarded to the correct target software component through the HELIOS Unification Bus. Dynamic class method generation is allowed in the Information System where a Smalltalk-based language is used. In the other components, the use of an early binding programming language (C++) does not allow this possibility. Helios also provides data-driven capabilities through the use of triggers in the Information System. No constraint programming is currently in use.

ADVANCED OO FUNCTIONALITY

A special software component, the Decision Support System, is dealing with rule-based programming while designing the Medical Logic Modules with Arden Syntax (ASTM E.32.15). The Natural Language Processor deals with Conceptual Graph using Object Prolog programming.

DEVELOPMENT ENVIRONMENT

Helios *is* a graphical development environment, including graphical browsers both for Opal/Smalltalk and C++. Starting with commercial Smalltalk browsers, the team developed their own dedicated browsers to accommodate contextual browsing. DECFuse and GEODE provide method tracing and debugging. For user interface development the project has used various tools such as UIMX and DEC Vuit. They currently use a home-made graphical user interface builder embedded in the Interface Manager.

STORAGE MANAGEMENT

The central repository is represented by the Information System where every atom of information is stored. As versioning is not completely taken into account in the GemStone DBMS, HELIOS team is implementing their own mechanisms together with a configuration management system.

CODE GENERATED

Automatic code generation is provided only in the Interface Manager. In this component, a graphical form design is automatically converted into a C++ class, to be stored in the Information system for further reuse.

PROJECT LIFE CYCLE

HELIOS is the brainchild of a consortium of researchers, doctors, and software developers from France, Germany, Switzerland, Sweden, and the Netherlands. Additional financial backing was provided by the EEC and Digital Equipment Corporation. The Medical Informatics Department of Broussais University Hospital assumed the direction of the project, under the leadership of Professor Patrice Degoulet.

Analysis and Design

The decision to take the object-oriented approach with HELIOS was based on several factors. The first is object technology's re-usability of parts, especially useful in a domain such as medicine. A medical environment might contain pieces of application code as well as medical object modelings that are exactly the same from application to application. Object technology provides the ability to build modules—both modeling and code—that can be re-used and customized in new implementations.

The second factor is the very nature of the medical information environment, which might include a wide range of media—test, magnetic resonance images, X-rays, CT scans, etc. Object technology was seen as the most flexible method for working with these complex data types.

Finally, object technology offered a means of modeling reasoning as well as data and processing. They needed to be able to model, for instance, the thought process a physician might go through when ordering a prescription for a patient.

According to Dr. Jean, technical director of the HELIOS project at Broussais Hospital:

> The need to manage complex relationships eliminated classical models from consideration, both for efficiency and ease of modeling reason. We needed to have a unique paradigm that allows us to deal with any kind of entities, and had the ability to manage objects the specifications or standardization of which are not completely fixed, without having to re-code the entire application when a format changes. In other words, we needed encapsulation and polymorphism.

Development

The HELIOS project was the first deep contact the group had with object technology. Thus, it took six to twelve months for developers to become confident with the technology. For A&D methodology, the team employed an OO method. When they began the project in 1989, there was no real mature OO methodology. They studied these different OO methods: OOA/OOD from Coad and Yourdon, Shlaer & Mellor's ObjectMaker, OMT from J. Rumbaugh, and Booch's Object Design. They currently use OMT with ObjectMaker after having used Coad and Yourdon for a while. They don't use a traditional V model of the life cycle, but instead a spiral model that reduces the time between specifications and coding, using successive refinements. The rapid prototyping general scheme was adopted for all the development subtended by the spiral model of the software life cycle. The three year project uses approximately 25 full-time engineers, this after the 14 months exploratory phase.

Deployment

Since the project is not complete, (the end of the currently funded phase will occur in December 1994), the only actual users of the Helios development environment are the members of the consortium. However, real medical applications are currently developed using HELIOS and are intended to be in production in 1994 in three hospitals.

Maintenance

Structures and procedures have been embedded in the HELIOS framework to facilitate the maintenance task of the generated medical applications. These structures are mainly represented by the Information System metabase where all the information concerning an object used in an application (documentation, application that has defined the object, applications that use the object, test procedures, etc.) is stored.

BENEFITS

HELIOS provides all the documented time and cost savings of object technology's modular programming and re-usable code, freeing developers to devote more time to other hospital projects. Object-oriented programming techniques have the potential to shave years off the development cycle for new programs.

It is difficult to give exact figures of HELIOS' quantitative benefits. However, project personnel estimate that the OO approach improves internal productivity by 50%. By far, the greatest long-term benefit is the more effective management of patient information. When physicians can access all the information they need in various media with one workstation, they can be more proactive in managing a patient's case. The patient receives better care, and the hospital is better equipped to control costs and use health care dollars more effectively, to the benefit of all.

CONCLUSIONS

Dr. Jean offers the following advice:

> Object technology is not as simple as what is claimed in the literature! You need a training period to become confident with the technology and to really use all of its advantages. Reuse is not given for free when using the OO approach. There is a cost of reuse: you must first design *for* reuse before being able to design *with* reuse.

ACKNOWLEDGMENTS

Participants in the HELIOS Program include:

BROUSSAIS UNIVERSITY HOSPITAL, Medical Informatics Department (prime contractor), Paris, France
>   Project Manager: Pr. Patrice Degoulet
>   Technical Director and local team manager: Dr. François-Cristophe Jean
>   Developers: Mr. Thierry Thelliez, Mrs. Dominique Sauquet, Mr. David Lemaitre, Mrs. Marion Lavril, Mrs. Marie-Christine Jaulent

CAP GEMINI SOGETI GROUP, Grenoble, France
>   Local Team Manager: Mr. Philippe Vauquois
>   Developers: Mr. Sergio Calabretta, Mrs. Christine Bernard, Mr. Philippe Gourincourt

DEUTSCHES KREBSFORSCHUNGSZENTRUM, Heidelberg, Germany
>   Department Head: Dr. Hans-Peter Meinzer
>   Local Team Manager: Dr. Uwe Engelmann
>   Developers: Mrs. Manuela Shafer, Mr. Andre Schroter

GENEVA STATE HOSPITAL, Medical Informatics Department, Geneva, Switzerland
>   Department Head: Pr. Jean-Raoul Scherrer
>   Local Team Manager: Mr. Robert Baud
>   Developers: Mrs. Anne-Marie Rassinoux, Mrs. Laurence Alpay, Mr. Pierre-Andre Michel

UPPSALA UNIVERSITY, CMD, Uppsala, Sweden
　Department Head: Pr. Werner Schneider
　Local Team Manager: Mr. Bengt Sandblad
　Developers: Mr. Bengt Goransson, Mr. Mats Lindt

LINKOPING UNIVERSITY, Medical Informatics Department, Linkoping, Sweden
　Department Head: Pr. Ove Wigertz
　Local Team Manager: Mr. Hans Ahlfeldt
　Developers: Mrs. Kristina Arkad, Mr. Nosrat Shasavar, Mr. Hans Gill

DIGITAL EQUIPMENT CORPORATION, Cooperative Engineering Center, Amsterdam, The Netherlands
　Department Head: Mr. Anwar Osseyran
　Local Team Manager: Mr. Ron Verheijen
　Developers: Mr. Caspar Jagerman

Recommended Reading

Harmon Paul, and Hall, Curt. *Intelligent Software Systems Development. An IS Manager's Guide*. John Wiley & Sons, Inc., New York, 1993.

Khoshafian, Setrag and Abnous, Razmik. *Object Orientation: Concepts, Languages, Databases, User Interfaces*. John Wiley & Sons, Inc., New York, 1992.

Ibid., *Intelligent Offices: Object-Oriented Multi-Media Information Management in Client/Server Architectures*. John Wiley & Sons, Inc., New York, 1992.

Pinson, Lewis J., and Wiener, Richard S. *Applications of Object-Oriented Programming*. Addison-Wesley, Reading, MA, 1990.

Taylor, David A., Ph.D. *Object-Oriented Technology: A Manager's Guide*. Servio Corporation, Alameda, CA, 1990.

Ibid., *Object-Oriented Information Systems: Planning and Implementation*. John Wiley & Sons, Inc., New York, 1992.

Winblad, Ann L.; Edwards, Samuel D.; King, David R. *Object-Oriented Software*. Addison-Wesley, Reading, MA, 1990.

Wirfs-Brock, Rebecca; Wilkerson, Brian; Wiener, Lauren, *Designing Object-Oriented Software*. Prentice Hall, Englewood Cliffs, NJ, 1990.

Index